C000089536

Spinner Magazine
Worldwide

Volume 8   Nov 2019

Spinner Magazine Worldwide

November 2019

IN THIS ISSUE

Dave Henderson

Editor Notes:

The Cover of #8 is a hen owned by Keith London and it's not the best photo but considering others I was looking at it's pretty good. Most use phones now for photos and these tend to be good when there is good lighting but not so good in poor lighting.

I hope you all enjoy #8 as it has been a work in progress going back many MONTHS and it's tough at times to get Guest writers, but appreciate it when they come. I just hope you all enjoy and I look forward to hearing your feedback.

If you need to contact me for any reason, please do;
daverollerpigeons@gmail.com

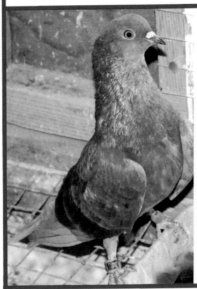  

Developing a Hen Family
What is Involved

The 3 Hens behind my Family

DNA UNDERSTANDING

There has been a lot of articles in recent years discussing such things as its related to the Hen pigeon in relationship to Mitochondrial DNA and with other genetic data about the W Chromosome coming out in the near future with new DNA software, I am kind of excited to see what they find out. Most will tell you to not read too much into these things, but when they start pointing out specifics of what the traits are you can't help but be hopeful. I just have a gut feeling that, at least in the Rollers, that this plays a more prominent role then we are aware of.

The Racing Pigeon world seems to be keeping up with all the latest genetic trends due to a lot of speculation about the qualities that a female/hen can contribute in a mating in the competitive animal "industry". I am sure many Roller fanciers have read about some of this data in recent years but I have yet to see anyone correlate this information in regards to it with the Birmingham Rollers as a competitive breed in regards to high velocity spinning and kit competition. I am not suggesting that no one has written on this topic in regards to the Birmingham Roller but if they have, I have not seen it. This genetic data is all relatively new, but the Racing Pigeon and Racing Horse world is paying a great amount of detail to this data as I will discuss more in this article below.

As the technology improves so does our knowledge of genetics as it pertains to specific animals and when it comes to money making industries like Horse Racing, Dog Racing and even Pigeon Racing they are always looking for a new angle to increase their odds of winning. The Birmingham Roller is not really a money-making type of environment but for me this is what makes it a much more rewarding one, because when a lot of money is brought into something it tends to corrupt the field of events that take place and creates more enemies than friends. I am not saying it is a bad thing to win events like the World Cup because we all know that this is the greatest achievement the Roller World has to offer. I am just saying when money is involved the people winning the most are the most hated.

As I read through this very thought-provoking article written by Silvio Mattacchione of Canada titled **"Mitochondrial DNA and the Significance of the Maternal Line"** I could not help but see the correlations that would greatly benefit the Birmingham Roller as a performance pigeon. Here is a link to his article via my personal website if you are interested in reading what Silvio has to say; **https://dave-henderson-rollers.jimdosite.com/articles/** I really didn't like the format in which this article was written that much but after about page 10 this article starts to get pretty "juicy".

Here is a straight to the point quote I hope you will appreciate from this same article;
"It will come as a surprise too many that understand why only mothers pass Mitochondrial DNA on to their children. All of your Mitochondrial DNA is identical to that of your brothers and sisters, your mother, her sisters, their mother, their grandmothers and so forth. Your whole maternal lineage can literally be traced back to the beginning in this fashion. When a cock mates to a hen the cock supplies the sperm and the hen the egg however since the Mitochondrial DNA of the cock is contained within the tail of the sperm and since the tail falls off as the sperm enters the egg it is impossible for the resulting offspring to carry anything but the Mitochondrial DNA of the hen or the mother. Now think of this when you are planning your mating every time a cock mates to a hen other than his sister or mother or other female member of his mothers maternal line he is in fact creating a NEW hen line each and every time."

Here is a quote from Professor Anker that is also taken from this article that I felt was very relevant and will explain very quickly the significant of a hens Mitochondrial DNA which directly influences the "vitality" of ALL her descendants via her and directly related females; **"Pigeons with excellent vitality recuperate faster, they are quicker**

able to form new reserves in the kidney and liver, and as a result of this, also get back in shape faster."

As Anker states here in this short quote, these great birds (hens) are able to produce higher outputs than your average bird and then recovery from a heavy workout is much quicker. The reason for this is that their organs function more efficiently and these are the top qualities you can obtain by using a very good foundation hen. Granted he is making reference to a Racing Pigeon with their racing but in terms of endurance and stamina the very best Birmingham Rollers are second to none. The birds do two different things but they are still needing a good system as described to perform at high outputs. Some of these birds might spin 30 times (or more) in a 20-minute time frame and this can really wear them down if their system is not running optimally.

This information presented here is new to me but as far as I can tell it has been talked about in the Racing Pigeon world for at least the last 8 or 9 years. I have been driven to do even more research after reading Silvio's article. I hope I am able to obtain more information in the near future so that we can better confirm this data that was discussed in this article by Silvio.

After developing a family from a Foundation hen over the last 25+ years there are certain things I saw transpiring in this process and this data helped to confirm some of the things that happened during the process of me creating this family.

I know this does not really cover all the details in regard to this topic. The article I reference can assist more on this and I am sure the book that is available at Shewmaker.com may help as well. I am just wanting to keep this as short as I can and give ideas and possibilities on these concepts. Not all birds will be developed equally and results will also vary a lot from loft to loft. Like they say there is a bit of luck involved with this stuff and you can never foresee what will happen until it does.

Some of the more recent DNA stuff deals around a gene they have found in the majority of the top performing pigeons and there are labs now testing for this specific gene. If you want to read more about this genetic identifiers check out Shewmaker Genetics; http://www.shewmaker.com/ There is a brand new book being released soon that will cover a lot more than I mention here. I am kind of curious about even testing one of my best Rollers to see what it shows.

OPEN YOUR EYES
When I first envisioned this hen line concept it was really like an awakening to me back around 1989. I don't know if others would see it the same way that I did but this is partially why I am writing this article to clear up some of the things on this subject.

A strong tendency I was seeing back then and still see today at many lofts is the simple fact that many fanciers are simply creating more high-quality hens every season then cocks. Many have told me that good hens are a dime a dozen but good cocks are hard to find and worth their weight in gold when you get one. I would ask these specific guys **"Why do you say this as it's a fact or something?"** They really have no straight answer and only mention that all the experts say the same thing in the various literature they have read over the years. We all can only hypothesis what we think and you never know anything about your OWN birds until you try it first-hand. I know where these outstanding cocks come from and am here to tell you that's it's from these outstanding hens we see in abundance and once you start on a path of line breeding to an outstanding hen you can be almost certain about the quality of the cocks that will eventually be coming through a hen breeding system.

So, if we are naturally seeing a greater number of high-quality hens in your program why is this happening do you think, because we need to try and analyze why this is don't, we? I would estimate from memory that over the years, that around 75% have said to me that they get more high-quality hens than they do with cocks of the same quality. When I look at this personally it is telling me that hens are somehow more dominate in their genetic makeup as it pertains to the Birmingham Roller's behavior, because if they weren't why would this happen, but at the same time why do others have a total shift with more good cocks?

Maybe it's about how they are designed and have a more balanced body because of how they lay eggs and produce young. I mean is the body balanced differently in comparison to cock birds? I know much of this rolling is part of an illusion and shape, wing length, body feathers, body length, neck length etc... can play into what they look like when spinning. I have expressed my view on the type I prefer and this type is a preference based on what I have seen over many years.

I have come to the conclusion that many of the factors that we see at various lofts are at play with type. No loft has the same exact system and even with the same genetic backgrounds they change over time based on selection at each loft. The different lofts can also develop different types of mutations in their own gene pools unique only to that family with their breeding methods; more inbreeding tendencies and line breeding methods all based around specific selection processes and these will evolve completely different.

Some might choose to just mix birds around amongst each other each season and never try to create a REAL family. Others will be completely content with this method by just constantly bringing in new birds and mixing with something else and the mixture of sexes at these lofts can vary from year to year, but in my case where I have been line breeding and inbreeding to the specific hens primarily I am naturally seeing more hens produced from my pairs and in the reverse if you are line breeding and inbreeding more to cocks you will begin to see more good cocks produced in your loft and just more cocks in general. This seemed logical to me when thinking about it, but why it happens genetically I had no idea. I came to this conclusion after getting some Hannes Rossouw birds that came from South Africa. Hannes line breeds to key cocks these has a tendency to produce more cocks.

I have recently been looking through some referred Racing Pigeon books and this seems to be well documented in this breed of pigeon that the more a common ancestor appears on a bird's pedigree the more prominent the sex of that particular bird will show itself in the stock loft. **(The Strain Makers by "Old Hand" 1995 page 12)**

I have chatted with Hannes and look at his pedigrees from his 2010 imports and he tends to favor red check cocks in his program, and has "Foundation cocks". His foundation cocks change over time but they are all closely related. His program can be very progressive too with him breeding young, flying them and breeding some of these in the same season. So, when I started breeding these birds', about 4 years ago, I immediately started seeing more cocks in my kit boxes in comparison to hens from these HR pairs. I have had some pairs that have produced me 4 rounds of babies and 7 out of 8 ended up being cocks. These cocks would also develop a little quicker than the hens on average, which is also the opposite of what I see. It was from my experience breeding and flying these birds that I came to this conclusion having access to his pedigrees.

What I have written here is what I have seen in my own loft and the evidence is very apparent. I am curious if others have seen different or similar tendencies at their own lofts, if so please feel free to contact me and let me know what your findings have been. I know that all will get varied results but they are interesting to hear about all the same. I will continue to do research on this topic and see where it takes me.

ENVIRONMENTAL OR…

As we look at the reasoning behind more lofts having a larger number of good hens in comparison to cocks, can this tendency be environmental and partially genetic because a cock bird has a natural desire to want to pair up to a hen that is receptive to him. These cocks can even be targeted more easily from the birds of prey because of this urge they have. We see birds pairing up in the kit box but most are unable to lay eggs because the environment is not supportive of egg production, even birds of the same sex pair up at times, like with two hens. The old saying is when you start to see eggs in your kit boxes you are most likely over feeding your birds. So, what I am saying is that cocky cocks can be a real pain in the butt and possibly they are getting culled for their natural instinct to pair up when they lose sight of flying and performing with the kit. I have seen a lot of cock birds like this over the years and the ones that start to have a tendency of flying out of the kit, no matter how good they spin and this might be the cause for having less good cocks – because they get culled. There are many fanciers that keep both sexes separate and fly full kits of cocks and full kits of hens as hold overs, but I am not one of them. The cocks I keep must be able to stay focused and keep their composure when flying in the kit.

I know that in some cases like with Ted Mann, 2015 World Cup Winner, he was able to identify specific culls not long after weaning them from the nest. I have seen a few of these myself and they tend to be larger baby birds (probably young cocks) that are very hard to get flying. These birds even seem to sexually mature faster than usual also. I can't say if this is just something that was part of Ted's birds or if this trait came directly from Hannes Rossouw from South Africa, because Ted's birds all had at least a small part of Mason blood in them.

My friends Tim and Daniel have also seen this tendency is some of Ted Mann birds and we have come to call this a "lazy" gene. Interesting enough Ted even speaks of the type in his birds being everywhere from very small to very large and everything in between. He also culled a huge number of birds and also admitted to me that his best birds where his hens. Ted said they were superior to everything he had in his loft, the very best performing birds anyway. So many of the hens were super stars with all the best traits you could ask for.

It is my view that I prefer having more hens, especially as hold over birds, in comparison to cocks. This choice has nothing to do with breeding a hen line, because I just recently discovered these tendencies list above (since my 2015 breeding season). My desire to breed a hen family had everything to do with what I saw and continue to see in the hens from my family or Rollers that is outlined. So, creating a hen family is just the best of both world to me personally. Hens are much more reliable, easier to manage, more well behaved on average and this for me means a more productive system with my limited time. I am not suggesting that I don't keep cocks at all because I fly them in mixed kits every year, around a 75% to 25% ratio. I would just prefer to have kits with the majority being more hens and less cocks. The cocks can be almost territorial and the more of them in your kit box the more chaos you have in your kit. This same chaos can contribute to how they fly, but many think its stress that can bring out the best performances with our birds. I would say on average my comp teams would usually have around 5 cocks in them on average and most of these are the well-behaved type.

One of my biggest pet peeves is having problem birds and when you have a lot of problems the birds won't kit and fly properly. Your kit can't score points if you have too many out birds all the time. We need to be very selective in our stock birds so you can eliminate these same problems, because they are at least in part genetic traits. We see guys flying the same birds that don't kit over and over again thinking that they will somehow get a different outcome each time they fly these problem birds. Problem birds create more problem birds when you breed them, it's as simple as that.

In the Racing Pigeon world many practice the "Widowhood" method of racing and swear by it. This method has you pair up birds and then once the hens lay eggs you take the cock away and send him to a race and the idea is that it encourages these cocks to get home quicker to their mate. So this also is a sort of stress on these cocks with this method.

PROCESS EXPLAINED

If you are able to breed and fly 100 Rollers each season and you don't have the space or time to breed and fly more, but would like to be more competitive in the flies, what do you do? You develop a breeding program that is going to improve your percentages of good spinners and I think the most effective way, in my opinion, is to develop a hen family. Of course the other method is most certainly to purchase some better birds, but I find that most just never put in the REAL work with their current stock to refine them.

As prescribed earlier in this article we have seen the significant of a hens' Mitochondrial DNA as it pertains to vitality in our best pigeons. Scientific studies are now showing that a lot of this vitality in our pigeons comes directly from the hen. If you build a family around a superior hen, you can keep this amazing vitality in all your birds by line breeding/inbreeding to this hen.

They have not yet mapped out the DNA to find where the "Roll Gene" comes from in our birds and we can only assume that it comes from a combination of genes that mix well within a specific pair. We need to harness these genes from a superior pair by a combination of inbreeding and line breeding. By all accounts I have seen it's a little smoother process to use the hen from these type of pairs because of how the genes are passed along to the off spring.

As we know a male pigeon has two Z chromosomes and a hen has a single Z and a W chromosome, unlike how sex is determined in humans with the male being responsible for this, in pigeons and birds, it's the female species that determines the sex of its babies. We also know that a hen is only able to pass her single Z chromosome to her sons. The cock in the pair is carrying two Z's and you just never know which Z will be passed on and I think this is where the inconsistencies come from, unless it's from a mother – son pair. We know that the hen passes her Z to EVERY son so we know her son is at least half of what she is so the odds increase that the son will produce birds more similar to the mother and if this mother – son pair is a hit pair I could only assume what she is, coming through this son (her mate) in high percentages of the time.

If we take this another year while taking a son off this first mother and son pair and pair it back to mom again then we can be more certain it's going to be like her but on the down side of this combination you might also see some negative traits pop up so I would generally not immediately progress to the next inbreeding right away, but instead put his hen on another cock from another one of her sons that was paired differently to continue experimenting with her. The more cocks you find that work with her the better off your program will be moving forward and I would prefer to pair up at least a full sibling pair off this mother – son pair and see how that goes. You must remember that type is very important in a full sibling pair because the odds of them taking after your foundation hen is more certain, but you never know until you try. Some birds nick together and others just don't for whatever reason.

You can develop cousin hen lines simultaneously with the hopes they will be able to mix these amongst each other in the end and that is where the "Pretzel" system comes into play that I have discussed in the past.

My own experience was taking this original son back to his mother (foundation hen) and then getting a handful of dynamite hens and then bring 3 of them back into the stock loft to put on everything else that was related. This spread the genes out a little bit more without having the do more inbreeding after hitting on this mother son pair that was so potent. After this initial year everything that were 1st cousins were used back and forth to discover breeding tendencies in them all.

It was around 1997 that I discovered that there was a genetic heart defect coming from one of these 3 sisters from the original mother – son pair. These were mentioned in this article as possible mutations in a hens' Mitochondrial DNA. I was amazed when I say this mutation listed having created what I created.

Here are some examples of faulty or mutations to the Mitochondrial DNA as presented by Freddy Vandenheede taken from this same article;
"EXAMPLES OF THE IMPACT OF FAULTY (MUTATED) MITOCHONDRIAL GENES
General: Small stature and poor appetite
Central nervous system: developmental delay/intellectual disability
Progressive neurological deterioration, seizures, stroke-like episodes (often reversible)

Difficulty swallowing
Visual difficulties, blindness and deafness
Skeletal and muscle: floppiness, weakness and exercise Intolerance
Heart: heart failure (cardiomyopathy) and cardiac rhythm disorders
Kidney: abnormalities in kidney function"

Interesting enough I find that nestmates tend to be closely related just like with twins. So, if you get a dynamite bird it's very possible that the same genes that made this bird good are also in the nestmate, especially if it's a "twin". A twin is two babies that are nestmates and also of the same sex. I would encourage you to experiment with these "twins".

There are many documented cases of specific individuals creating winning lines of Racing Pigeons all breeding around a single hen and several cocks. You can literally go for many years with just 3 or 4 birds that work together, 30 plus years easy enough. This same article discussing Mitochondrial DNA also goes to talk about how many can get very lucky with specific pigeons and creating a perfect environment for a winning combination and Silvio states that **"Good Pigeons Make Master Breeders."** Just let this statement really sink in.

The biggest thing I see with many out there is just keeping too many pigeons and not fully testing what they have before getting more. Many appear to be more of a "collector" of good birds from various fanciers and not anyone that will be able to develop a tight network of key genetics in their pigeons that can do it all for you. I must say there are many documented cases however of top flyers never developing their own family of pigeons and would only cross birds over and over just to win races or competitions working a "NUMBERS" game. Which means breeding a lot of birds and the cream floating to the top.

The old saying still plays true here; **"You can lead a horse to water, but you can't make it drink."**

MY EXPERIENCE
Some have stated that you can do this entire process with a cock as well, but it's my opinion that the hen breeds much truer to herself in comparison to a cock and I have had better results using a hen. The genetic make-up of the cock having two full Z chromosomes I think has something to do with this in terms of inconsistencies, but I am not a geneticist so I can't really speculate on why this has happened when I have tried it. All I can do is tell you what the process was for me when I followed it.

I am not saying that I have not tried to create a "COCK LINE" using similar techniques because I have, several times. What I am saying is that when I used an exceptional cock I created, flew and attempted to create a line using the same processes I have used with my hen lines and I had much more inconsistencies and lower percentages of good pigeons with the cock lines. Yes, I produced a few dynamite birds with the combinations I have tried, but overall the percentages remained lower when trying this system with cocks.

The process I describe is using a dynamite cross cock in comparison to a hen of the same. If cocks are already part of an existing proven family this is not necessarily going to yield you the same results. So, building the line I am describing and you concentrate on the hen exclusively until you find a cock that is prepotent in this mix. The cocks and hens over time begin to be very much equal but you will still get more hens produced than cocks. You can't discover any of these things unless you are actually breeding birds, you can't really predict outcomes with any breeding pairs until you try them. The top producing cocks that come from this type of systems are very good birds and as you know much easier to mix and match to other hens in this program as the birds are all very much related, but they also tend to mix well with non-related families as well.

I developed an amazing cock with a cross mating and he was superior in many ways to your average bird. However, when I attempted to develop a family around him nothing seemed to work, as I had hoped. I would breed him back to one side of the family that was new to me and nothing much to write about, some descent birds but nothing I could consider stock worthy. Then I put him back to the mom side, not to his mom however, and I got better results but again not good percentages, but did produce a true standout out of around 14 babies. So, one stock worthy birds in 14 are not very good odds in my view. Had I put him back to his mom I would have been again breeding back to the hen and I wanted to do the opposite.

The following year I take this outstanding daughter back to the dad and see and the same results, one super star out of 10 birds produced and flown. I would have thought in my own head that I would suddenly begin to see some better percentages but I didn't. I would have preferred to try what I was comfortable doing by putting this outstanding cock back on his mom, but I was trying to work it without using the mom at all, because for 1. she was a recessive red and I did not want to start producing a lot of recessive reds and 2. I wanted to stay the path of pushing to build this line just off this outstanding cock without any direct influence from the mom. I went on to pair him to his moms ½ sister who was blue and still poor results.

As I go through my last 3 breeding seasons and while switching pairs around with some of the key birds' I was hoping to see results from with multiple mates, you can see some tendencies that stand out. You are trying to find specific birds that have produced on multiple mates. I have seen two hens that have produced good birds on 3 or 4 different cocks over the last 3 years. These breeding hens' standout and the results are even better than I had trying to line breed this cock listed above. The cocks I like the most have had only good results off just a single hen during the same time frame.

The only knock I can say is that I have been unable to survive a lot of birds and can only evaluated young up to the point of them being taken by predators. I have possibly found two "Click Pairs" as well using one of these hens mentioned above and two other hens with specific cocks, but these cocks did not show similar results with other hens, yet. I had tried to further test the one hen but she suddenly stopped laying consistently and I need to treat her with an ovarian infection before I can begin to test further.

So, as I go through my records and check where birds are coming from everything leads back to specific hens. I don't know how to explain this but it's the same for me when I begin looking at what and how many of my best kit birds are hens and how many of them are cocks as well. The survival rate of the hen is higher, they screw around less and stick to business when they are kit birds in comparison to the cocks that will sometimes develop a cocky attitude and this can subject them to birds of prey taking them or even being culled for their bad behavior.

As I stay true to the same and that is constantly going on in my own head; **"Like breeds Like"** this kind of guides me in the right direction to stay the path into developing birds that do what I want and at the same time spin and fly like I am desiring them to. Every year is still a work in progress and some pairs just don't work as expected. If it was this easy everyone would have world class Rollers.

This is why I look for the signs, I see what the birds give me and all things point to the hens. Even with proven, already developed lines or families where cocks and hens tend to be more equal in performance, I am still seeing the producers as HENS on multiple mates. What would this say to you? To me it means focus more on the hens and their babies. It will just take time to learn the breeding tendencies of them.

I know that you can look at the same thing from multiple perspectives and to some degree or another you can see data on all sides, meaning in some instances we see the opposite. But when you take a cock and hen that breed and produce like a "Click Pair" and then move them off to other mates over multiple seasons and you are not seeing the same results with the cock but seeing similar results with the hen on multiple mates I can't help but notice this.

*These **"PRODUCER"** hens are similarly seen in the Racing Pigeon world and also used to the benefit of some that pay attention to things like this.

There are many out there that I have asked about how they have developed a family of Rollers and none that I can think of developed a hen line like I have. I can't even say any have even attempted it. However, many are and have developed COCK families using Foundation cocks. I have asked several of them why you didn't go to the hen to develop the line and several I recall told me if you do breed like this the birds get small and weak over time. *(I have seen the same suggestions in some Racing Pigeon books)* I said "have you tried it?" They said NO. I don't want to name these people here but I am sure they are not alone and I know for a fact they aren't. It could be a society type of question where some look at "MALES" as the dominate sex with more strength when we know that this is not always the case with our pigeons, but these biases do exist in the same manner as they exist in people.

I know this is not some fluke because some out there have actually done similar things I have, in developing a family based on a single hen and had a lot of success with this. I have in the recent months been going through Racing Homer literature to see stories of individuals that developed families based from stand out hens and they have even shown this tendency with the top breeders and flyers that if they had long term success with the Racers they are consistently producing top racing hens when the vast majority are only racing cocks with the widowhood method.

If we look back in the History of our Rollers even a couple very notable birds in Pensom's era were 514 and the Red Headed hen. Both of these were hens and have been spoken of for many years but did they actually breed tight families based on these single hens in a family? I have no idea but non the less we still talk about these hens after many years. So again reference to more hens.

If I go on to counter what some said about why they don't build a family of hens because it will lead to a weak family of birds, I can do nothing but laugh a little, because this can be nothing but a false statement. Yes, there are weaker birds found in all families, small, weak immune systems but you must refrain from using these birds, even if they are outstanding performers, in your breeding program because **"Like breeds Like"**. As I have noted several times above you have to pay attention to TYPE.

I have gone through my breeding loft several times to weight my birds because at the time I did this I had read some article discusses such things and I wanted to see what my birds' weigh. As I have mentioned several times my birds are very uniform in size and type across the board and I found these same results when I went to actually weigh them. What I found was that the cocks and hens only varied approximately 1 ounce and that even the birds I thought were light because they were very small were not in terms of weight. My cocks always ran from 8-9 ounces and the hens 8-9 ounces. The hens tended to be on the lower sides of these numbers and the cocks on the upper side of these figures, but I had NO birds that were 10 ounce and no birds that were 7-ounce figures except babies right out of the nest. So, it's completely fictious to say the birds get weak and super small when you line or inbreed to hens. I have been working a HEN line since 1992 and the birds are the same as they were in the beginning in terms of type. As I said you can get some small hens at times that appear very small but they still have good muscle mass to them and will actually fill out nicely once they are stocked.

If you have selection processes that encourage weak birds, like only making them fly for 30 minutes or less you could experience some issues I feel because unbeknownst to you, you are actually creating an environment that is creating weak birds. I personally want ALL my birds to fly and perform for at least one hour and this type of bird is strong, has a lot of endurance and stamina.

To me we are striving for the birds that can spin around 30 foot all the time and perform with a frequency of about once or twice per minute. Now envision what this bird would need to look like. These birds need to be muscular, not weak and lacking in body. They can't be too strong and muscular however or you can get opposite results. The birds must have good balance with a particular body type that can fly for an hour and still perform at least once per minute. It's a special bird that can do this type of performance and creating a full kit of them will never be easy.

Good muscular birds are better able to out fly the birds of prey and they are also not going to disqualify you in a kit competition, but again with too much strength and too much control and we have a Racing Pigeon.

Our pigeons are very much habitual and once you condition them to do things, they will do them consistently even if they are fed even just slightly less than they were the day before. I demand my birds to fly between 1 to 1 ½ hours. The only time they might fly under an hour is during the molt and If they fly beyond this time frame it's time to cut their feed back a little. There is a fine line between too much and too little and there are a lot of reasons why; weather (hot and cold) and molt being the largest issue of these.

STARTING A HEN LINE
After combing through the reasons above about why it will be beneficial to develop a Hen Family when talking about Mitochondrial DNA benefits, let's jump into how we get started and why I think this is the fastest and best method to move forward in developing a reliable family.

If you are looking to start and develop any family of birds you are really needing to be very selective on what birds you use in stock. Selection means everything when it comes to creating the best birds you can so always follow strict methods of selection.

This hen, for this breeding program, should be your ideal bird in every way; super high-quality spin, frequent and a superior kitting pigeon that works well with the kit. It's my opinion that you want front-breaking birds, birds that want to lead the kit. We know that most kits fly in a circular formation so they all can't be front birds but the genetics are also not the same in every bird produced. This type of bird will race back directly to the kit with an amazing drive to be in the kit. Birds that follow an order of dominance will break more in larger clusters because they are looking for a "sign" by the lead birds to break. Solo performing birds that are continually breaking from the back of the kit will seldom perform with the group and these birds will also cause your kit to turn in circles. So birds that are breaking from the back of the kit encourage more waterfall breaking. All of these characteristics are genetic and part of selection so don't think they aren't.

It is well documented that you only need a single potent pair of birds to get going with and only one top hen. You should ideally want one hen that works with several cocks. We have seen this happen over and over again in the Racing Pigeon world and continues to happen even today. You take sons of these top hens that perform very well and do everything right while sharing a very similar type as this hen does. I think type is the key to making these pairs the base of your foundation and also birds with a natural ability to replicate. I am not saying that you can't get lucky using a mediocre son but if you cheat yourself in the beginning it will probably show up later on in the development of these birds.

I find it's best to create multiple lines at the same time that are cousins to each other and this will jump start your "Pretzel" breeding program and it's with this program that you build on your long-term reliability. Don't be afraid to experiment with various combinations because really nothing is out of bounds when you are developing a family of birds from a select group of Rollers.

I have several articles on my website about how to work a "Pretzel Breeding Program" so please visit for more information on this. https://dave-henderson-rollers.jimdosite.com/articles/ I think you will get the idea once you get through the information. This article kind of compliments this information.

Making any family good is all about selecting the right birds to work with and finding the right combination of genes that can be reproduce after the initial mating is the hardest part. It might not happen in one or two seasons and it could take you closer to five years before you find just that right mate for this fantastic hen. It is also possible that you never find a "click" type of mate for this hen until you pair her to one of her sons. We can never predict these kinds of things and I am sorry to say there are no short cuts in getting and creating a family of top performing Rollers, because we can never predict how the genes will mix early in the mix. Many may not even identify the bird(s) do to their own personal biases that they have and may not even know these biases exist with them.

As outlined above my suggestion would be to find a son that is as close to your ideal pigeon as you can find off this key hen and then pairing him back to his mom. If all goes well you will see some good quality spinners to select from and then be able to stock up at least 3 or 4 birds off this key pair. In the book "The Strain Makers(1995)" the author suggest finding a "Producer Hen" and pairing it to the best cock you can find in the hopes to producing some exceptional pigeons, even if you have to borrow this "Producer Hen" or "Best Cock" and sharing the babies with someone else. In this combination you fly all the cocks and stock up all the hens to breed from and try them out.

I cannot really know exactly what this author is thinking in this process, but the key is in the "Producer Hen" so this must pass through her Mitochondrial DNA or her W Chromosome in theory because a hen gives her W Chromosome to all her daughters as well as her Mitochondrial DNA.

When you think you have your ideal hen to build a family around it is wise to find another bird that will work with this hen. The obvious choice might be this cocks ½ or full brother or even HER ½ brother with a common mother. Most don't realize that you don't need a lot of birds to establish this "family" and it's probably better you don't have a lot of birds. The less distractions you have in your loft the faster you can progress. The only downside is putting ALL YOUR EGGS in one basket so it's always best to work several lines at the same time so that you won't get caught with your pants down. This means only working this hen with say 2 cocks and thinking it will automatically work. You might need two or more high caliber hens to work with at the same time that might even be related.

The main issue as I see it is to not worry about competing in events like the World Cup until you have build-up your stock loft. This entire equation depends on the amount of time you can spend with your birds, quality time. If you can maintain more pairs than your average fancier can and properly fly out all the babies you could possibly have enough birds to compete in this process in comparison to the small-scale breeder with a smaller focal point.

You will however need to not worry about competing in events like the World Cup until you have build-up your stock loft with enough good birds to create competitive kits every year after a specific time frame. Losing key birds that would benefit your stock loft will set you back at least one season and the bird might even have become a game changer in your program, that you only see in 1 of 100 or more birds produced. If we lose a lot of birds to the birds of prey these key birds might never survive to even be realized. So, don't be this kind of guy and take care of your stock loft early so that you can have good kits every year.

I hope this article gave you some ideas of how to build a family of birds around key hens and gave you the insight to make wise decisions about what to do and how to do it.

The advantages of a hen line are obvious and let's not forget that your birds will naturally produce more hens (around 60%+ at my loft) which are easier to manage and are much more reliable as kit birds. This might be why they do better as race birds also? The birds will be more similar in type and size and will also produce much better percentages of good birds and will eat and act the same. In the Roller World and with competition, the more GOOD birds you produce the more reliable your kits will be each year. It should be a goal to have hardly any REAL cull pigeons and you should only lose birds from the birds of prey and only get rid of them to make room for the new crop of babies coming up through the ranks each year.

If you want to discuss any of the topics covered please feel free to contact me through my website or send your emails to; davesrollerpigeons@gmail.com

References;
The Strain Maker (1995) by "Old Hand"
Mitochondrial DNA and the Significance of the Maternal Line by Silvio Mattacchione
The Basis of Breeding Racing Pigeons by Leon F. Whitney

A 2019 Roller Pigeon Documentary by Milena Pastreich
For updates on where to see the film follow us at facebook.com/pigeonkingsfilm

Extremely Deep Rollers

Jurie Ferreira with the 2017 South African National Record - 38.53 seconds Roller

2017 Longest Roll

Position	Club	Name	Ring No	Seconds
1	NLDRA	Jurie Ferreira	NLRA / 24 / 2016	38.53
2	WRDV	Sakkie van Staden	WRDV / 201 / 2014	13.65

We have all talked about breeding and flying deep Rollers at some time in the time breeding and flying the Birmingham Roller breed. Some prefer really deep birds but really deep to one is not really deep to another. I witnessed some high-quality deep rollers in my time, since 1980, but the vast majority I would say do are nothing close to what we will read about in this article. Most of the really deep birds referring to in this paragraph are in the 40-60 foot-range, or 3 to 5 second spinners, but this article is not discussing these depths which are more common with most fanciers around the globe.

I was able to see some very high-quality EXTREMELY deep rollers bred by an old friend here where I live in or around 1990 so I can only presume that there are others. These birds were of very high-quality and would perform a solid spin from around 100-200 feet and pull out. These would normally pull out of the roll less than 100 feet from the ground and then head back to the kit slowly. It could take several minutes for them to get back to the kit and most of these birds might perform like this 2 or 3-times before they would be exhausted and land even if the majority of the kit was still flying.

I handled several of these birds I witnessed on multiple occasions and they were large birds similar to a smaller than average Racing Homer, but much larger than the average

Roller that most of us fly. I would estimate their weight at around 11 to 12-ounce, or more, birds. The quality of their roll was undeniable and the only problem is that all of them would eventually end up killing themselves less than 3 months after starting to perform. If I could estimate the duration of their roll, I would say they were performing for around 7 to 10 seconds.

Looking back on these birds and how they were managed I would have to say they were definitely mishandled. These birds were flown regularly and probably not fed properly based on the amount of energy they were using for these deep spins. I would say they would probably need 3 to 4-days rest to recuperate and rebuild their energy reserves for such a high stress performance and I know now that this did not happen for these birds. I think this could be, in part, of what caused their early demise, but I am still not convinced it would have saved them. I have seen a lot of birds develop similar to this and with high quality only to end like this at some point.

I just know that with the experience I have with rollers now that high performance extreme velocity birds will be so tired after a flight that they will not even feel like eating after they land for several hours and the vast majority of the fanciers expect them to eat right after they enter the loft and trap. If you were feeding birds individually in their own cage and allowing them to rest prior to eating you would not have the same issues but the majority of us "flock" feed our kit birds and this means some will naturally eat more than others do and the hardest workers will eat much less than the none performers even. On some of my best spinners over the years I would have to give them at least 2 days rest for them to keep up long term and even then, some would never be able to retain enough muscles mass to keep up these performances several days a week.

I had read an article in the National Birmingham Roller Club that took place in South Africa, in the mid to late 1970s. There was an organization there in South Africa that bred for extreme depths and if my memory serves me correct the National Champion at the time, when Ken White was there to witness it, was a 27 second roller.

When I started to do a little research, I discovered this organization in South Africa is still active today.

A LITTLE HISTORY

Ken White imported the birds to South Africa in 1953 (their literature states) and they would go on to call these birds the "Kent Strain". Ken White was a UK citizen that lived in South Africa similar to how many in the U.S. live in New York and move to Florida during the winter months, having two homes.

As the story goes these birds were originally judged by the British standard for kit competition format in which the birds would normally roll for 1 to 2 ½ seconds and needed to display a specific type of quality to score. Some of the birds would roll much deeper than you would normally see for kit competition and these would be culled for not being able to stay with the kit good enough. These deeper cull Rollers would end up getting the attention of some that would go on to create a club specifically for deep rollers and today these birds are called South African Distance Rollers.

It appears this trend was much more popular back in the 1960's in comparison today. The Eastern Districts Roller Society was the major club for these deep Rollers that started in 1948 and was disbanded in 1966. The Deep Roller organization then became the South African Roller Pigeon Federation until 2017 when it was changed to its current name the South African Distance Roller Federation. As you can see in the September 2019 results below there is at least 4 clubs that are competing on a regular basis with the SADRF for about 8 months per year on average. The birds can only be flown on clear days so that when the judges come to each loft to judge their 5 bird kits the birds are easily marked and identifiable to the judges.

The birds in each kit are scored for 15 minutes and the scores recorded are a combined total of all 5 birds in the kit. Each bird flown will have a separate judge and stop watch in hand. Each judge uses a stop watch to record the duration the birds roll and there is an Umpire on hand from the SADRF so that they know the judging was sanctioned and the fly followed the rules. Below you can see the rules that all clubs must fly by when flying in this competition.

A bird must perform for at least a 1 second roll to be recorded and each bird doesn't not get a combined total of seconds they performed, but the entire group of 5 birds is tallied using each birds' best time. A bird can only get a higher score if it performs a longer roll than the one previously recorded. The longest duration of roll per bird is recorded and the duration in seconds are added together to get the total on the day for a specific fancier representing their club.

They told me during this research for this article that the average duration on the best birds is around 7 seconds and the average number of rolls for an individual bird during the 15 minutes is 4 rolls. The bird must roll, fly back to the kit and then perform again. There is no accounting for the quality of roll only the duration the bird must perform. The birds cannot twist (plate rolling), nose dive during or do anything that is not a standard type of roll – backwards summersault. They must roll and then pull out of the roll before hitting the ground. I have seen video that was taken from drone footage that displays a bird performing 16 seconds, but it never pulls out in the video so it could have just been a "loop" that went over and over, not 100% sure at this point.

The club secretary confirmed to me that they contract in drones at times to get good video of the birds but had not done this in recently. I was wanting to ask them if the drone pilots could confirm them on the altitude they are flying when they perform. This information did not come back before writing this article.

I asked them the process of judging the birds and if they use binoculars to spot the correct bird using a spotter. They told me binoculars are banned and that the birds must be marked or colored in such a way that the judges can easily identify the birds so they can't be scored because a judge won't be able to see the birds in question good enough.

I also asked how high the birds flew on average during the judging and I was told there was a lot of conversation in recent years because in 2017 a bird broke the record with 38 seconds and pulled out very low to the ground, some thought the bird might have rolled from 2000+ feet up. I would guess 38 seconds had to be more around 900 to 1200 feet off the top of my head, because I have had birds roll down from about 350 feet that were moving pretty good and these were about 12-15 seconds. I know from old experiments that it's virtually impossible to tell the color of a bird at 2500 feet up, you can see it but it's only a DOT.

I learned about the heights of the kits several years ago when a friend's son in law used a drone to fly up above his kit of birds and video tape them, he had to set a maximum height on the drone due to FAA regulations and that was set at 450 feet. This drone was large and about the same wing span (18-20" square) as a Roller pigeon so it gave me a nice relationship. This really blew me away because if I would have guessed how high the drone was, I would have said 600-700 feet. Back in the day I would have estimated 400 feet was more like 600 feet, which a big difference of 50% higher than I thought, so I think you could easily think 1200 feet was 2000 feet.

I know that many will disregard this type of bird but I think it's something to develop them that are roll in greater depths and still pull out before hitting the ground. These are not the type of bird I am interested in personally but as a Birmingham Roller Hobby I think there is room for all types of interest in this flying breed.

The National Birmingham Roller Club also hosts two contests; the 20-bird kit competition and the 11-bird individual contest. They are judged differently and this gives a better view of what is out there. I personally think the rules on both could use some updates but they are what they are right now.

I want to thank the officers at the SADRF all their helpful information and I wish them all a great season for 2020.

2019 Longest Roll

Position	Club	Name	Ring No	Points
1	BRA	Dijon & Jackie	SADRF 0506 '19	15.28
2	CDRC	Frikkie Aucamp	SADRF 0562 '17	14.89
3	BRA	VJ Govender	SADRF 1893 '18	13.13
4	BRA	VJ Govender	SADRF 1874 '18	12.78
5	BRA	George Small	BRV 1273 '18	12.69
6	BRA	VJ Govender	SADRF 1893 '18	10.69
7	BRA	George Small	BRV 1326 '18	10.60
8	BRA	Dijon & Jackie	SADRF 0506 '19	10.50
9	CDRC	Frikkie Aucamp	SADRF 0113 '18	10.25
10	BRA	George Small	BRV 1270 '18	10.13

September 2019 Longest Individual bird score

September 2019 Competition Results

Position	Club	Name	Points
1	BRA	Dijon & Jackie	34.92
2	WRDV	CC Troskie Lofts	34.63
3	NLDRA	Andre Stolz	32.14
4	NLDRA	George Small	31.57
5	WRDV	Carel Laufs	30.51
6	WRDV	Sakkie van Staden	30.33
7	BRA	Lesley Johnson	26.59
8	WRDV	Alwyn Grobbelaar	26.18
9	CDRC	Frikkie Aucamp	25.40
10	CDRC	Jan De Kock	25.23
11	BRA	Johan Geyser	22.84
12	CDRC	Chris O' Riley	22.56
13	NLDRA	Bean Broderick	21.74
14	CDRC	Ryno Aucamp	19.88
15	NLDRA	Johan Booyens	19.87
16	WRDV	Chris Kinnear	17.85
17	NLDRA	Dirk & koos	16.66
18	BRA	Vijay Govender	15.25
19	NLDRA	Dawid Pretorius	12.03

20. COMPETITION RULES

20.1 The duration of a competition will be fifteen minutes.

20.2 All the members of a club will compete on the same day, unless a member qualifies for are-flight.

20.3 Clubs are allowed to fly two or more panels with the understanding that rules 20.2, 25.1 and 25.2 applies.

20.4 Score Sheets must be handed in at the first person on the competition route.

20.5 Participants are allowed to hand in two Score Sheets, but they must choose which Score Sheet to use before start of the competition.

20.6 A competition kit consists of five (5) pigeons, and only one (1) reserve pigeon is allowed.

20.7 A participant has five (5) minutes after releasing his pigeons in which to shout "time" only then will his pigeons be judged

20.8 Every roll exceeding one (1) second will be recorded as a roll score. Only the improved score will be recorded on the Score Sheet, judges must call out every score, where the score is not an improvement the score must be called out followed by "NO IMPROVEMENT".

20.9 A pigeon may only be judged if it forms part of the kit, or when itis within the five (5) minute "TIME" period after rolling or leaving the kit.

20.10 No score will be afforded to a pigeon that cannot be positively identified.

21. FLY RULES

21.1 Pigeons must fly for the duration of the competition to be awarded one (1) bonus point for flying.

22. GROUPING RULES

22.1 Any pigeon leaving the kit in the first ten (10) minutes of the competition gets five (5) minutes to re-group before itis awarded two (2) bonus points for grouping.

22.2 A pigeon that rolls between one (1) and five (5) seconds in the first ten (10) minutes of the competition gets five (5) minutes tore-group before it is awarded two (2) bonus points for grouping.

22.3 A pigeon that rolls between five (5) and ten (10) seconds in the first ten (10) minutes of the competition gets seven (7) minutes to re-group before itis awarded two (2) bonus points for grouping.

22.4A pigeon that rolls ten (10) seconds or longer is automatically awarded two (2) bonus points for grouping irrespective if it re-groups or not.

23. ROLL DOWN RULES

23.1 Where a pigeon rolls down in plain sight for the duration of the competition it has (5) minutes to take flight undisturbed before it is disqualified for rolling down.

23.2 A pigeon that rolls down behind an obstruction has (5) min to reappear before it is disqualified for rolling down.23.3The roll down rules MUST always be applied in conjunction with the GROUPING RULES.

24. SETTLE RULE

24.1A pigeon that settles forfeits all points awarded to it. This includes a pigeon that has rolled down, took flight in the allowed five (5) minutes as per rule 23.1and 23.2 but then settles

PIGEON COLOUR	CLUB RING NO	YEAR	IDENTIFICATION	NO	JUDGE	ROLLING POINTS							ROLL	FLY	GRP	TOTAL

SCORE SHEET — SADRF

The SADRF is a member of SANPO and SASCOC

COMP NO: 4
PARTICIPANT: Gc Small
MEMBER NO: KO13525
CLUB: BRA
ROUTE NO: 2
DATE: 16/06/19
TIME: 8:36
POSITION: 1/6

PIGEON COLOUR	CLUB RING NO	YEAR	ID	NO	JUDGE	ROLLING POINTS	ROLL	FLY	GRP	TOTAL
Skede wt Dubbel Geel	BRV 1280	2018		1	LESLEY		rolled down			
Witte Groen Vlerk	BRV 1270	2018		2	NICO	8.48	8.48	1	2	11.48
Witte Roos Steel Stomp	BRV 1309	2018		3	Jaco Missed	9.03	9.03	1	2	12.03
Witte Green vlerk Stert	BRV 1326	2018		4	Eric Missed	9.16	9.16	1	2	12.16
Skede wt als Blou	BRV 1273	2018		5	Tyron Missed	9.09	9.09	1	2	12.09
Check wt Geel Stert	BRV 1253	2018		RES	Lesley Missed	6.00	6.00	1	2	9.00

TOTAL SCORE: 56,76

JUDGE 1 ___ JUDGE 2 ___ JUDGE 3 ___
JUDGE 4 ___ JUDGE 5 ___
PARTICIPANT ___ UMPIRE ___ CLUB CHAIRMAN ___

September 2019 sample Score Sheet

South African Distance Roller Federation

Home of the Distance Roller Pigeon

EXECUVITE CHAIRMAN
Carel Laufs
secretary@sadrf.co.za
+27 79 519 9119

WEBSITE
www.sadrf.co.za

TREASURER
Frikkie Aucamp
treasurer@sadrf.co.za
+27 83 605 8898

SANPO

Find us on Facebook

WORK EXPERIENCE

Progression through Selection

There are some things we do as pigeon breeders that will assist us in this process and it's something we have to work at and its thru good record keeping and proper management that we hope you can stay on a path to success. It's not going to be an easy road but I can assure you and if you are persistent and passionate enough you can accomplish nearly anything you set your mind to do in regards to flying better rollers.

In order to get moving forward we need to approach our pigeons with a scientific method. This means keeping records on the pairs, what babies come from these pairs and evaluating the outcome of these pairings. We need to both track good and bad traits in these pairs, not just the good birds. I also find it is very good information to track the various losses we experience as well. Some birds just simply learn how to survive and this is all part of this process of evaluating our birds. Keep records and never trust things to memory and the easier your system is while still remaining accurate is the path you need to follow. The more birds you breed the more data there is so this is why I suggest keeping things on a manageable scale so you don't get lost in this process, manageable to me may not be the same for you.

The whole process of progression is a normal process in life especially for the fanciers choose to raise the rollers in a way that you can be successful in the end. This is simply to do the best they can with the birds they have and to develop them to something extra ordinary. In the end, you will find that this is also going to end up being the most rewarding part of this hobby, but this is up to each individual. No one can make you follow the steps needed to be successful, you need to do this on your own. The old saying is *"You can lead a horse to water, but you can't make them drink..."* So basically what this means to a roller breeder is that you have to want to be better and do better and this process all starts with educating yourself to do what is needed for this to happen. To me there is nothing better than matching up a pair you like together, flying the young and then seeing them become good spinners that you can be proud of.

We don't progress with the usual good birds we progress with the extra ordinary ones. The programs that are the most successful across the planet are the ones that are developed from a select number of "key" individuals. It does not happen just because you want it to, but you can get lucky from time to time. It's line breeding to key individuals that gives you the ability to progress.

The steps we take in progressing our rollers is really just a state of mind, it is like being self-motivated and having a desire to do more with these rollers and envisioning the path to get there. It's really the path to get there that can hang up many of us as we really just keep **too many pigeons.** Keeping too many pigeons is one of the worst things we can do if we want to be successful with the ones you have. What is too many pigeons? Well a good rule of thumb might be if you are able to keep track of all the birds you have, fly them with little effort and be able to manage the birds in a way that will benefit them and your program then you probably have the right number, but if you are culling birds on a whim, can't properly band and record the birds you are breeding and find errors often in your records then you probably have too many. These numbers will not be the same for all of us.

A manageable number for me is keeping 12 pairs or less, breeding and flying around 80 birds a year. The fewer I can keep and fly the better the birds generally do under my management system. I just personally don't want to make the birds a JOB that I can't escape from. I want it to be enjoyable and there is a balance to anything in life and it's finding that balance that will be the most rewarding to you.

There are many reasons why fanciers keep too many pigeons. I think firstly they feel the birds are just valuable to them and yes many of them they might have paid some good money for and just don't feel good about throwing money away. Some fanciers just like to collect birds from various families out there to say they have some, others just don't feel like they can properly assess and evaluate them until they have had them 4-5 years in their stock loft on many different mates and the list goes on. Whatever the reason is you really need to be disciplined enough to *"bite the bullet"* at times and move forward on an educated guess to simplify things in your loft, if you keep too many birds for too long then you can let your best birds sit for too long. We keep records so we can track progress and this gives us the ability to evaluate breeders.

I personally can't see myself keeping on to a pigeon for more than 3 seasons if I have not seen a fair number of good spinners come from this bird. What is a fair number? I would say at a very minimal figure would be 1 in 5 or 6 produced early on and if I am seeing multiple birds each year that are getting my attention then I might be onto something. At some point you need to analyze your situation and you only want to progress your program with birds that are extra ordinary. This can also mean particular birds working on multiple mates that can produce a larger percentage of good spinners in comparison to others you have in the stock loft. I have personally had pairs that were so good together that they might actually produce 100% good breeder worthy spinners but I was not able to label them as such only due to some birds being lost one way or another, usually to the predators.

Well you might ask *"What is extra ordinary in comparison to your normal good spinner?"* This is a good question. I would personally say that your ordinary good spinner is something you see pretty often but is without a doubt good enough to breed from and might very well produce fantastic pigeons for you, but when you see them spin you look in AWE! The bird that I am talking about can take your breath away when you see it perform and will also appear to be nearly flawless in its execution EVERYTIME it spins. When we see a bird like this it burns into your memory forever. Again this caliber of this bird might not be the same for all fanciers *(especially if you have poor eye sight)* but for me this bird simply put looks like a spinning ball up there whether is shows a hole or not. These birds will perform like a *"Yoyo"* up there, they spin out fast and return to the kit fast and appear to enjoy what they are doing. They perform with such speed that it's is impossible to guess how many revolutions they do during a single spin without using high speed video. Many might even reference these birds as looking like a blur and will descend *(drop altitude)* slower than the normal roller does while performing. Many birds of this type will rarely spin beyond 20 or 25 foot but their ability is undeniable. These same pigeons do all this and are never a problem in the kit. They kit tight, always perform in the kit and develop over time like clockwork.

After breeding birds for many years you will find that breeding and having birds that are capable to reproducing good birds is the direction you need to go in. Sometimes these extra ordinary rollers fail to reproduce themselves. I find it especially beneficial to find a full-sibling or even the nestmate of this extra ordinary pigeon that is also a good spinner and stock it up as well. The sibling actually might end up being the better producer for you, but you need to experiment with this in your own loft. You will discover over time that **all birds are not created equal** and you need to remember this. Successful lofts are found mostly on key individuals that we line breed with.

We can have top spinners that at times will never reproduce spinners which seems very odd to me and we can even at times have birds, for whatever reason, were not flown out that end up being some of our best producers in the stock loft. The birds either have it or they don't, this means genetically capable of replicating good spinners. This is the key to the whole equation to progression, having a line of birds that are capable to reproducing themselves.

Some might think this sounds easy enough to do and theoretically it is just like anything else, a process of progressing your birds it just takes time to find these birds. It's just easier said than done and certainly can't happen overnight miraculously just because you want it to. This whole process takes a lot of work and persistence to progress your birds, but it will happen if you want it to. Breeding rollers takes time, so you have to stay focused on specific goals to progress our birds from year to year, the word is *"Baby steps"*. This is the best we can do and if you are not in the birds for the long haul then it certainly won't happen.

Much of what we do simply is about putting in the time to discover outcomes. If we just fly the birds and never observe them while flying, we are missing out on the majority of the important information we need to properly evaluate them. We need to see what their tendencies as the old saying is **"Like Breeds Like..."** If you don't watch them during the evaluation period you are just doing things lazily which will not end well for you in the long run. We need to know the birds like the back of our hands so we can know what to expect from them in the future. Even minor developmental things will haunt you later on if you don't pay attention. This could include being too frequent, flying out of the kit too much, coming down early and the list goes on. These are serious flaws assuming that they are completely healthy while having these issues.

No doubt a big part of this will be how long it takes the birds to develop into spinners and much of this has to do with home much air time they get as very young birds. It's hard to judge the birds if the problem is dealing with you not being able to properly fly them so they are able to develop properly. Many times birds if they are not flown can even prevent them from developing altogether, especially cock birds as they will lose focus on flying and focus their attention on breeding which will force you to cull many of them. Had you flown them regularly and kept these birds on proper diet this might not have happened and thus you ended up culling a bird that may not have really been a cull at all, you just simply neglected it. The bottom line is if you can't properly fly them in the neighborhood of 5-6 days a week you will really not be able to evaluate them and progress your gene pool to the next level.

Developing the roll is almost like riding a bike, the more you practice the sooner and better you can do it. Over time it will even become a 2nd nature to you and this is the same for our rollers. This is not to think there will not be any mistakes along the way, we just hope these mistakes don't CULL them at the same time – via bumping or rolling into hard objects. All these facets play into our bird development even your work schedule.

Considering all the above you might even need to evaluate what family of birds have work with even. If you can only get birds out 3-4 days a week regularly birds that might take 5-6 months to develop under normal daily conditions might take a year or more and like I mentioned many may not even develop properly causing you to cull them. So you might be better off finding some of the 3-4 month developers that might develop within 6 months with minimal flying. No matter what you decide to do or breed the birds will all eventually develop the way you have made and selected them over time. So someday down the road if your schedule changes and you are able to fly the birds more you will again run in to development issues and have to alter things all over again. It's just the nature of things.

I talked with Jerry Higgins after he retired and he was experiencing much of what I mention above. He went from flying 4 days a week to flying 7 days a week and this played a huge part in how the bird developed. He told me more of the birds began to get too hot with more flying and this caused him to change his game plan. So as I mentioned your schedule plays a big part in the birds' development good and bad.

The bottom line is that we progress our lines through select individuals, not hordes of birds. We want to breed a higher percentage of good spinners not just MORE birds and get lucky here and there with our mating's. You are on the clock as soon as you stock a bird and if you are not able to utilize them as best you can while they are stocked then you are kind of wasting your time. We just can't assume that our birds will live to be very productive and leave a long-lasting impression in our lofts. A lot of this is how you use the opportunities given to you. The time you have to develop a line around key birds is very limited and you can't take any of it for granted.

It is my idea to start small and then build up over time with only good spinners that you can be proud of. This happens very slowly at first and we need to select only the very best birds. We need to gradually increase our breeding numbers from these key individuals and this is where you need to stay focused. Refrain from getting too many birds whenever possible so you can keep things more simple to evaluate the birds you have properly. It's real easy to just breed birds and then toss them to the side for others and start over. However it's an art form to develop birds to your liking and make them extra ordinary. If you do it long enough you can really do some positive things but these things take time and if you are not patient enough it will never happen for you.

You only need a few key birds that are able to produce high percentages of good spinners to make a reliable line of birds. You can start with as few as 3-4 birds and breed for a very long time with just these few and have a lot of success. Many assume you need a whole flock of good birds to win such events like the World Cup but this is not true in the slightest. One thing is set in stone you have to learn how to fly and handle the birds you have and learn to get the most out of them in terms of performance. You need to become a good flyer to be successful in this sport of flying rollers. It will not happen for everyone as many just do not pay close enough attention to what is going on.

I hope that you all are able to get a little insight from this article and I welcome your input, until next time...

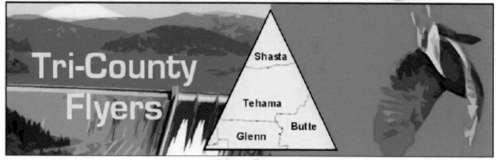
In The Spotlight

Interviews in the hobby

Keith London main photo Pigeon Kings Documentary

Meet Keith London

Hello I am Keith London and I am 55 years old. I currently live in Los Angeles, California. I started getting really serious in to Rollers in 1988.

Where did birds came from (what sources) and how long been working with the line(s) you have? (Please give details)

I got my first birds from several sources. These birds came from Rayvon Hall, Kevin Adams with my main foundation coming from Sanford Johnson or "Smoke". The bird from "Smoke" is in all my birds.

You say all your birds come from Rayvon Hall, Kevin Adams and your main stock hen came from Sanford Johnson and that your main hen has now been bred to everything you have?

I don't have the Rayvon birds any longer. They were weeded out through the normal selection processes. The hen from Sanford Johnson was Smoke herself, and I acquired her mother before I even got my Smoke hen. Smoke, her siblings and several generations off her are responsible for the infusion of her blood into my program.

What year did you incorporate the Sanford hen into your family? How was her performance?

Smoke was actually the start of everything I have in terms of my family of Rollers right now. This all started in the 1991 season. At the end of each season these birds were always the best I had in my kits and I only had 4 pairs of them, so they became the center of my entire program.

Do you fly with a specific roller club? how long, list other clubs you have flown in over the years?

The most recent club I belonged to was the Top Performance Roller Club (TPRC). I have belonged to the Inner City Roller Club (ICRC), West Side Roller Club (WSRC) and The Roller Association (TRA) over the years. I helped form the West Coast Roller Club.

Would you say your current family of birds (the sources they come from) are of a similar in background to each other? if so, please describe how.

The current family I am working with is a mixture of several lines in a unique mixture. My base is from Smoke and I have blood from Juan Navarro, Arnold Jackson and Don Norwood. I have also introduced one Norm Reed cock and several birds that are Jerry Higgins blood. Johnny Smith has been very influential to the creating of my family.

What qualities can you say you are breeding for? Please describe with as much detail as possible on these characteristics in your family.

Well I will put it like this; the Smoke birds are the base of my family and everything has gone through them. These birds set the kitting, homing instinct and speed or velocity. The Norwood birds I have used gave me the stability and type. The Jerry Higgins/Norm Reed gave me the commitment to depth which attributes to better depth multipliers and bigger breaking for competition. After pairing the birds together I will breed them according to their individual performance. If a pair produces me short spinners, I will then put these back to the Johnny Smith birds. If a pair produces me deep spinners, I will put them back on the Smoke blood. All the birds have been fully integrated into a real family but some sides of the family have a stronger influence than others do.

You mentioned your whole family is integrated. Does this mean you run various lines within your line of rollers based on the blood mentioned or do you just always mix

them however you see fit to? (You do or don't keep "cousin" lines within your family?)

like I said, "I used several birds to cultivate my strain of rollers for two reasons, (1). To be more competitive (2). For my own personal goals.

How many birds do you estimate are behind your family of rollers?

There are at least 5 individuals that are responsible for contributing their specific traits to my family. Those birds are Smoke, Bull eyed Spangle, White Heat Cock, #89 & #730 (which are both of the Norwood strain,) and now Platinum which was implemented in 2009. The Weapon cock and hen have also contributed a little but a significant to this family. These birds have had to work with my stock that is 75% or more of the Smoke blood.

I notice your main hen is a grizzle, do you get a lot of grizzles due to this hen in your loft?

I get some recessive red grizzle and torts mainly, but not a huge amount. I also get dark checkers and blacks in these.

Are you getting the qualities you are striving for in your current birds or are you still looking for something better?

I would have to say that everything is working and moving along as planned.

Do you keep more than one family of rollers? if so describe them and why you have multiples.

I have only one family of rollers due to my family being totally integrated.

You mention you usually have 28+ pairs breeding but this year only 12? Are all 32 from this family you developed outlined above?

Each pair is expected to produce to the same degree, even though it doesn't work out that way most of the time. Depth is the only factor that I don't expect to be the same. Speed, style, unison, and frequency of those factors I expect to be the same or close to the same with all of my stock pairs.

How many babies were you raising with 32 pairs per season and how many did you lose?

I would raise between 50 and 60 birds in each round, and I would let the birds go 4 rounds. I would lose at least 40 from the birds of prey. I would give away about 20 to shows and other donations, give some to friends and sell a few. I actually train for myself about 90 – 120. I would be lucky to have 2 ½ kits into the roll by the end of the season.

How long do you fly out a roller before you stock it and do you breed all year long?

I try to fly out all my birds for at least two seasons. Most birds have a better chance of me stocking them from the nest if I've flown several siblings of from this pair with "GREAT" results. I usually breed from February to September.

Are you still experimenting with other out crosses regularly?

In regards to my regular family of rollers as described above and I am no longer looking to mix in or bring in anymore blood to this family. I am completely content with my progress and as I refine them more, I expect things to continue to improve for me.

I am also working on a side project outside of my normal family that is developing an Almond line. A friend of mine is handling this line and I am assisting him.

Who are your closest roller friends? how long have you known them.

Rayvon Hall was one of my closest friends before he passed away last year. Rayvon and Bruce Hall I have been friends of for over 20 years now. Juan Navarro and I are still very good friends even though he is no longer in the hobby. Kevin McCray and I also continue to be good friends today.

How does your family of birds develop? describe how they develop in detail and what percentage of roll downs do you see on average each season.

As a general rule of thumb my birds start coming into the roll from 3 to 5 months of age on average. I would say they are not mature at this young age and are usually at their best after the adult molt and going into the second season. I would estimate I get around 4 to 8 roll downs per season.

What type of pairings would you say work the best for you? Cousins, half sibs, mother-son & farther – daughter etc.

I very rarely do mother and son or father to daughter. Most of my birds are cousins now any way and related by way of 2 – 4 birds that are common to my flock.

If you could describe the "type" of bird you like or in your opinion has been the best over the years how would you describe them in your own terms? (example: short stocky, broad chest, tail and flights are close to the same length, type of body in the hand etc.)

The apple body is very consistent in my loft. I like the birds with a little length, wide in the chest, medium depth in the keel, short secondary feathers, and a tight tail that appears as a single feather.

You mentioned the Norwood blood is from 3 sources and then Reed, Higgins and Smith birds are also similar in blood lines (back ground)?

Yes, the Reed/Higgins birds are used in the same way at my loft. I don't have either in my loft right now except for my Platinum Cock.

I know that Higgin's new line from the early 1990's came mostly from Norm Reed are these the ones you are referencing too in these? And of course Smith's birds have a lot of Higgin's influence in them, right?

Correct

You mentioned you have 12 pairs in your loft this season? How many of these birds are breed by others and how many by you?

Platinum is the only bird that was bred by someone else other than me I am using.

You have less birds because you are currently unable to fly? Are you feeding your babies to other fanciers to fly for you?

I am currently sharing a loft with a friend and this is why I only have room for 12 pairs this season.

Do you have bad losses to the BOP where you are? give details as much as possible?

My losses were very bad in 2017, which was the last year I flew. Couldn't train youngsters because of the Coopers and had a hard time keeping them once they got up due to the FALCONS!

Did you notice the BOP are around less at any certain times of the season?

The birds of prey are worst in the beginning and the end of the season, although I get hit all year when I fly. I have to fly less often after September.

Do you think that the yearlong flying in that area has contributed to more and more BOP's over the years?

Well, I haven't flown all year since 2003. I always try to fly until late September. But there are some guys that fly all year. Most of them are not in clubs though.

Do you think there should be an organized effort to maybe have all the clubs lock down at a certain time during the off season?

Most clubs and members lock down around September each season.

Do you write articles for your local club or group in your area? I see you have authored a book? Details.

I used to write all of the articles for WSRC. I used to write for QSDC Magazine and Bird League Magazine. Yes, I have a book published called "NALANNI 5".

Have you seen this New Castle virus going on in your immediate area? what are your thoughts on this.

I think they are going about it all wrong. First, they should've controlled the wild pigeon population since they go from place to place throughout a day. The quarantine was not specified in my immediate area.

What has been your best breeder(s) for you with your current family of rollers? do you have pics of them? Can you describe their aerial performances and are they good breeders that were also top performers?

My hen #1135 Recessive Red Grizzle has been my best hen for the last 6 years.

Describe that area where you fly? town, average weather.

I live in South Los Angeles. The weather here is usually mild to warm at best. Rains sometimes and cold weather don't last long.

Do you work with any specific fanciers as a team, to develop your birds and theirs? if so describe.

I haven't in the past but I have a group of guys I'm working now.

**On a side note to Keith London he was the center of a new Roller Documentary called Pigeon Kings that was released in 2019. This documentary is currently traveling around to various independent theatres and screening. The photos shown in this interview were from the movie project and I was giving permission from the Director and creator of this movie named Milena Pastreich.

Milena tells me to keep a look out for this movie in a town near you and by following the movie on their Facebook page; www.facebook.com/pigeonkingsfilm/

photo by
Shaughn
& John

**It has been a real pleasure doing this interview with Keith and he was very forth coming with all the information you find here. He is a real asset to our Roller Hobby and I am really looking forward to watching "Pigeon Kings" in the future. I am sure many of us are.

I hope that conditions improve for Keith so he is able to fly his birds more regularly but with the on-going New Castle Quarantine combined with the heavy migration from the Birds of Prey all you can do at times is keep the birds locked down and force them to hunt elsewhere.

A Young Henderson cock trying out in stock for 2020

Thinking Outside The Box

Reading Our Rollers

There has been a lot of discussion over the years about looking at our best rollers and seeing something in them that maybe others don't see, special qualities that only some can see. These subtle qualities are not easily seen. This is a very controversial topic and it's pretty much on the same page as the "Eye Sign" topic that some talk about. In the end much of what is seen in these concerns has more to do with a specific family of rollers and not so much of a UNIVERSAL characteristic(s) we see at all lofts.

Many might think it's some sort of trick and I think there is some merit on both sides of the fence depending on the individual. As Bruce Cooper says in an article that he wrote about such things that appears on my friend Arif Mumtaz's website titled "Bill Pensom's ability to Judge" from 2004. You can find this article at this link; http://mumtazticloft.com/default.asp

This article that Cooper discusses is about how it was said that Bill Pensom could "Grade" Birmingham Rollers on their performance ability off of characteristics he could see in them by handling them and looking at them. Cooper says that Pensom was able to do this so easily that he had a hard time understanding why others could not do it. I had heard that some fanciers would actually pay him to rate the birds from best to worst and assist in pairing up their birds and as Bruce Cooper says "It's obvious they must be balanced together in the coop".

I heard that Pensom traveled all over the country doing this sort of thing and I often wondered why? I personally thought this was very trivial to say the least. I mean what can Pensom really tell you about YOUR own birds that you flew and selected from the air for stock that you don't already know in regards to their performance? Do you see how ridiculous this sounds when he has never seen them fly like you have? I can only assume this was for notoriety of getting a "celebrity" like Pensom at your loft and having some sort of bragging rights about Pensom selecting your pairs for you. This type of behavior is very baffling to me.

In the basics, we look at birds in both type and genetics in them and try to blend them together to complement each other. Some like to balance for color, strengths and other things that we feel will create good pairs. I will a lot of times just go off a gut instinct and sometimes it doesn't work but I feel pretty good about it during the process. We just honestly can't predict how birds will mix 100% of the time and what the outcome will be overall. Granted this is the some of what makes this my favorite part of the breeding season, the planning stage.

I can say that I tend to be a critical thinking type and looking at things and analyzing them. I thoroughly think over most things and this is why I know many of these IDEAS are not something you can expect to work more times than it doesn't. I think it's all just an educated guess based on past experiences. I don't profess to knowing everything either but there are certain things that just don't make any sense at times and welcome ideas from others so that I might analyze this idea on my own.

I am not saying Pensom could not do some of what Cooper talks about in his article, but you just can't expect it to be some sort of "Magic Bullet" type of thing similarly to how I mention the "Eye Sign" topic above.

Many swear by eye sign, especially with Racing Pigeons, but as a good friend of mine told me one time it's more of a sign of the health to the pigeon and specific characteristics are just something that might work with a specific family of racers.   The basics is that if people are paying attention small details like eyes or feather quality, they are probably paying attention to many other aspects of their pigeons that the average guy isn't. Do these "traits" translate with other families of pigeons? Maybe, but certainly not all of them.

Early in Bruce Cooper's article he gives the impression that he KNOWS Pensom could do what he says he can and gives examples but then let's Pensom off the hook at the very end because he must also suspect that it won't work 100% of the time. As I and probably many others have pointed out about this specific topic, it doesn't take a "Brain Surgeon" to figure it out that it's a "trick" that sometimes works and many times doesn't.

I know it's not REALLY A TRICK, but it can seem this way. It's more of an intuition that you can develop over a period of time doing something. This happens with doctors, animal vets, school teachers, police detectives etc. This is what I talk about being a gained experience in a specific thing. Some might call this a "TOOL" of the trade.

I will now go over what I look for in my own birds and then we will come back to the heart of this article shortly.

A 2019 baby Henderson Roller

Now when it comes to identifying specific physical traits in some birds that I see on the ground I have learned to see this in some of my birds while they are still in the nest. This trait I have only developed with my old family of rollers that I have mentioned a few times in past articles. This is a LOOK I can spot usually while the birds still in the nest and it's what I call "EXPRESSION" and it is a specific look in the "FACE" of the bird (a head, eye and beak look). The unique thing about these birds is these birds are not scared of you, they might move back if you reach in towards them but they appear as curious about you as you are of them. The baby pic above is an example of a bird with the characteristics I talk about. The interesting thing is that most birds don't have this demeanor I mention (expression) as babies and we know that others can and will still develop into a good-spinners that are capable of making the stock loft and not display these characteristics. When I see birds like this, I am automatically drawn to photograph them even at an early age.

So what I am saying is that I know there are birds that exist that could have similar characteristics I mention here in other lofts, but do they mean the same thing they do in my loft. This is the issue with these methods. There is no assurance that you can rely on this method 100% of the time if some are thinking you can. My experience has shown me that there is no better way to get spinners than to breed out of them, **"Like breeds Like"**.

As many know I also have some South African import rollers and I can see some of these characteristics in them as well, but they don't translate into the same type of pigeon unfortunately. It's seen in good ones but also in ones that end up being full-fledged culls. I will need to keep paying attention to these birds and see if I am able to identify specific traits in them that I might be able to rely on in the future. I will keep you posted.

Here is short story about a Racing Pigeon fancier;

In an article titled; **"Mauricio Jemal - I Salute You!"** by Silvio Mattacchione published in 2016. This story tells of a Mauricio Jemal from Mexico. Jemal paid Piet De Weerd a large sum of money to scour the world to find the best birds he could to give Jemal a good start, he collected 3 pairs for Jemal. De Weerd had a unique method of rating pigeons that created good breeders that could win a high percentage of races, 70% or better in some instances. This was all done by holding the birds close to the body. Jemal taught himself a similar method and then went on to train 4 other individuals of his technique that were all living in the United States.

These birds were developed from over 50 years of breeding and Jemal never liberated them for over 30 years until he moved to his wife's hometown. He was not allowed to race in his hometown in Mexico because he won too many races. This didn't deter Jemal because he continued to breed them and select them by this particular technique he developed. De Weerd used a similar technique but had refused to teach others this because he made a good living grading pigeons. This method would allow you to breed sound birds even if not flown. Jemal was obsessed with the breeding of them and developing them and would not prefer to lose his prize birds in races if it was of the correct type. The found this characteristic in approximately 10% of the birds he bred.

Here is a quote in the article from Jemal; **"The hen is the key to your entire breeding operation. The hens are the keys to your success. The hens are the keys to your longevity as a successful breeder of racing pigeons. Without great hens, without exceptional hens, without a family of exceptional hens you will achieve nothing of lasting value!** and here is his theory, the open secret is that only females can pass mtDNA onto their offspring and that the Mitochondria DNA is the energy powerhouses of each and every cell in the bodies of every living thing on earth."

On a side note we know that hens (birds), unlike humans, have the ZW sex determination system, and the **FEMALE** (not the male) determines the gender of their offspring. In birds, the sex chromosomes are Z and W (not X and Y like in humans), and the male is homogametic (ZZ) and the female is heterogametic (ZW). I had wondered if the secret to the hens was in the W chromosome and recently inquired on this with genetic experts using electronic microscopes that are doing research today on this. I will write an article on in the future, but as of know they have not done a lot of research on the W chromosome.

So as you see Jemal inbreeds to amazing hens and they are the focal point of his breeding program and I guess In the Racing Pigeon world it seems possible to develop top birds without ever flying your stock birds, but there are many different families of Racing pigeons and would these techniques don't work on ALL racing pigeon families? I have no idea because I only raise rollers. The idea that this might be possible should motivate some to keep trying to find traits with your birds that are outstanding.

Link for reference to you all;
https://docs.wixstatic.com/ugd/efac56_d169c5cd2d0b40f2888e933cfffd06ff.pdf

In the Racing Pigeon world there are many that swear by eye sign and I read an interesting test performed in the book titled **"The Basis of Breeding Racing Pigeons"** by Leon Whitney from 1969. The author talks about knowing several in the UK that breed and paired up all their birds based solely on eye sign every year. One fancier mentioned had produced a couple of race champions.

As with all races many birds can get lost and end up straying into other lofts.

The author collected a bunch of lost birds, feed them up well and then invited of these experts in to grade some eyes of race birds he had, but never told the "eye graders" that every bird he would be looking at were LOST birds. There were several dozen available to be graded. There were many birds discovered with excellent eye sign and a few had very highly prized eyes, but every one of these were lost birds.

I suppose there could be other issues that caused them to be lost, maybe an illness that was not identified before racing and it could have been owned and exhibited by a beginner flyer. There was no way of knowing these things by just finding lost birds.

I mean the same could be said of birds that are entered into the infamous "ONE LOFT RACES" we see now a days. Guys would not pay big bucks to enter junk birds into these events but environment can and does play a huge role in how birds develop.

It is possible the many reading this could be the first-time hearing about such correlations we see in our birds. Maybe this literature will provoke you to pay a little more attention to the details of your own birds to see if any of these tendencies are present in your own birds because they might be there in plain-site, if you just pay attention.

I often wondered if eye sign was something that Bill Pensom looked for in the "breeders" especially when he would handle them, what exactly he was looking for in the birds specifically. I know I have not seen any notion made in regard to the eye clusters I have seen in my own birds during the Pensom Era writings that discuss "eye clusters" in the pupil (shown just below in this article). If anyone has some literature on the topic please feel free to email me a copy of the article. We are talking about literature from the 1940s to the 1960s, while Pensom was still living.

A specific feature that I have seen in my old family of birds is what we are calling "Eye Clusters". This photo (below) shows a bigger than average eye cluster seen in the pupil of the eye and every bird I have had with this characteristic has bred me spinners. The particular one in this photo is the father of my #1 Henderson hen who was dynamite in the air and also a good producer for me, but she does not show these clusters in her eyes, however. I can't say these cluster birds produce higher percentages than any others that don't possess this, but only that every bird that has shown this characteristic has produced me at least one stockable spinner. This characteristic goes hand and hand with the "Eye Sign" theory to some as mentioned earlier but again maybe this might not be a feature that others will notice as being any better than any others. My best birds I have had in stock that produced in high percentages did not have this characteristic.

Eye Cluster on a Roller

There are some other signs seen in the kit birds that are spinning good with high velocity that you might notice as well; frayed and worn down inner secondary feathers and also wearing on the bottom side of the #10 flight feather (very end wing tip feather). The edge of this feather could only wear as it does in some birds by rubbing with the other wing tip, hence the Shrunken "A" style which would have wing tip feathers rubbing on the full downstroke during the spin.

There are also varying degrees of a style that is between displayed styles as well depending on the bird in question. I don't think birds will perform with the same style every time they perform either and can even display a style that appears as an "A" with the peak of the "A" open and not quite touching. Our Rollers are just animals and are subject to being sick, feeling ill so we can never expect them to be a machine, even though some of them once in a while appear to be running off a high-performance engine, LOL.

Considering how controversial these ideas are I really just can't say if any of these things translate into working at all lofts with the same meaning and I would have to say with 100% certainty that these ideas won't work everywhere with all families of birds. All I can say is that I can look at other lofts and see birds that are my "TYPE" of bird and ones I tend to like, or tend to be good birds at my loft, but this is as far as it goes. If they are stock birds then I would have to assume they are also good spinners but what I have wrote here is all I can tell you about what I know on this topic.

I have noted often that our rollers are a WHOLE PACKAGE of qualities and not one dimensional like some talk about when it pertains to their spinning ability. It's a whole bunch of little things in them that make our best rollers what they are. The starting of the family begins with good quality hens that can reproduce with multiple cocks. This includes how they act, how they fly, how they perform and then how they produce in the stock loft, all birds are not created equal. However if everyone bred their birds with the same level of science behind them there might be many more real good families out there.

I must emphasize that there are no shorts cuts here and I have to select birds the old fashion way just like everyone else. We use trial and error and make the most of it. If you notice any tendencies you see test these tendencies further to see what works. We have to breed them, train them, fly them and select them from the air just like everyone else. However I might look for slightly different things than others and I especially pay attention to the style of my rollers which is why we do this right? Breeding and flying what we like. If we can't see the end results of the breeding pairs in the air than this is not going to be a something many of us will go for that are desiring a performance bird.

If we take a look at any fancier and how they select birds for the stock loft they have developed a system they are using to rate all their birds very similar to how I do for overall quality. In the Style Diagram seen below I display the only two styles I consider for stock birds. I don't like "H" or "X" style at all and will only use "A" or "Shrunken A" as I call it for stock. Some others might consider "Shrunken A" as a "Ball Spinner" but to me they certainly don't look completely round like a "Ball" and when you see the shape they have while spinning you would have to it is nothing even close to being round when style comes into play. The side view is the only thing in my view that looks like a "BALL".

Some out there might consider "H" a style better than my "A" style and this is fine but it's my opinion that if you breed for "A" style the overall quality of the birds will look better on average because you produce less "X" style birds. Selecting for style has to happen out of the gate and if you start with an existing family of rollers it might be tougher initially. This style is of course seen in the front and back view while the bird is performing, not the sideview. I will only breed from these two styles I list below and this is my preference.

I know that genetics plays into everything in regards to our families of Rollers and how they look. Some birds might have slightly longer wings, maybe shorter tails or legs. Some could have more body feather and even the way they stand naturally can be different in the various families. The interesting thing is that families tend to have very similar types from the cocks and hens with very little deviation, if they don't it's probably not a REAL family yet.

Other genetic traits can also include the way they fly, how fast they fly and how they develop in to the roll. These are all genetic traits that are passed along and eventually end up in your next crop of babies that you will eventually be looking at for your future stock. This is a cycle that keeps us going.

In my own loft EVERY bird has to possess virtually the same quality of spin using a system of how I rate them. A lot of this is just looking at them and knowing what they are and how good they are. You compare them to the best you have seen in the past and if you feel a bird of this particular caliber can help your program you keep your fingers crossed that it is still there when you decide you need it for stock.

I also use a PC pigeon program that allows me to develop my own rating system for my stock birds. This grading system has 10 qualities I use and some don't get a rating until I see their babies the first season in action.

Style [0 - 5] 4 minimum stock	4	80%
Velocity [0 - 10] 7 minimum stock	9	90%
Kitting [0 - 5] 4 minimum stock	5	100%
Depth [1 - 50 Max Depth	30	60%
Expression [0 - 5] + is Better	5	100%
Breeding [0 - 5] Potency + better	4	80%
Termperment [0 - 5] + is Better	5	100%
Overall [0 - 10] Overall Impression	10	100%
Prolific [0 - 5] + is Better	5	100%
X Factor Special Characteristic	8	80%

My #1 DH cock, 85% rating Overall

My best producing stock cock EVER only scored a 69 on this scale and he produced until he was 14, he was a prepotent bird in my stock loft and his offspring for other fanciers also. I added an "X Factor" category a few years ago to give these best birds, like the one listed above, in stock a little more recognition in my program. Is this type of rating system needed really? Not really but it's interesting when you see birds under the same system even though some that are rated lower are better producing pigeons in my program.

My rating system might seem to be more complicated than what others use, but it really isn't. It's just about using software I know how to use and don't want to change from as long as its working for me. The best feature is keeping track of my breeding pairs, you can record their babies in it, list your "A" team birds or "B" team birds, you can easily print up breeding records and pedigrees. Once you learn it you never forget it. You can make this program custom to your own likings just like I used this rating scale. The program is called Power Pigeon 4.1.

When I select birds for stock ALL birds must kit tight and fly correctly and be easy to manage birds. There is no room for bad flying and kitting birds in my loft. So what I am saying is that they must do EVERYTHING to my personal standard and kiting and flying has NO deviation in this equation what so ever. Exceptions might occur if a bird was ruined by heavy attacks brought on by the birds of prey. This can scare some birds so badly that they will never be the same, but some might think the hawks are now part of the whole equation and birds that are unable to adapt to this are no longer able to make the stock loft? I think there is merit in birds that can survive but on a high-performance based pigeon like the Birmingham Roller we also need to take a chance on a bird(s) like this once in a while. Who says you won't be able to find a happy medium by pairing this bird to a stronger bird with a balanced pairing?

From the screen shot shown above, you can see minimums to be considered for stock in style, velocity and kitting. To me a rating of 4 in kitting is a bird that never deviates from getting back but might take a bit longer to return in comparison to a bird rated a 5 in kitting that will jet directly back every time. Velocity is more personal to each loft it's the "accelerator" type that would be a 10, the ones that start fast and appear to shrink and gain more speed throughout the spin, then you down grade from there. So a 9 would be a very fast bird that is equally as fast as a 10 but doesn't not have that extra gear like the "accelerator" type has. The Top-Rated birds in our lofts are also the rarest birds you see if we look at it that way.

The fundamentals of how various fanciers select birds for stock are very similar I think but many don't keep records of the things I do and the stock birds I use will have some minor variations in velocity, style and of course depth. One thing that I can't afford to do any longer is fly stock worthy birds for 2 years, the best I can do now is fly for around 15 months on birds that are exceptional, but mostly it's due to the lock down in the winter that extends this. If I see a particular specimen that gets my attention early (before lock down) and it is only 8 or 9 months old and showing the qualities I need, I will not hesitate to try it. I mean worst case scenario you can put it back out to fly again after a few rounds of babies. You have to remember that birds we bring in for stock are not in huge numbers each year, we hand pick the birds we use in small numbers except for in the first couple of seasons you start. You need to evaluate those birds before you replace them for the most part, even if that is from a single mating from just one season. This process you do on your own.

I know the very best handlers and breeders of these amazing birds pay a great deal of attention to the details we see in our birds. The ones with the greatest ability to succeed can dedicate the right amount of time and efforts to doing what is needed to be successful. The vast majority are in a position of just doing the best they can with the resources they have due to the many life factors we have in our own lives. These factors change throughout our lives and most don't get the best of all until they are retired from working.

The birds of prey now play a huge factor in everything we do and if you are lucky enough to NOT be experiencing this particular issue you are very lucky indeed. I live in an area where the birds of prey are so bad that I am almost guaranteed to lose 40% without even thinking about it. I am unable to fly for 3 to 4 months of the year in the prime weather conditions of the winter months. This would be Winter and going into early Spring.

As we know there is no molt this time of year and the air is very cool, which are two things that are greatly needed when you are flying rollers and looking for optimal conditions with high performance conditions. If I dared to fly at these times, I would literally lose multiple birds every day I let them out because the birds are prey in this area are that thick during those times here. You might get lucky for a day or two but once they find you it's over. The wild birds migrate from the mountains when the snow comes and the birds of prey are forced to follow them or starve unless they can adapt in other ways. The pigeon fancier for the most part is sustaining these birds of prey in many facets of this process artificially which is very unfortunate.

I know that Pensom did not have to deal with these same issues in his time living in Southern California like they do today or he would have surely wrote about them.

As noted above it was said that Pensom would be called to various parts of the United States to grade and even pair up birds for individuals. I suspect this had more to do with notoriety and less to do with Pensom being an individual that knew it all. They could use Pensom for the betterment of selling their birds even, have pictures taken with him to show proof.

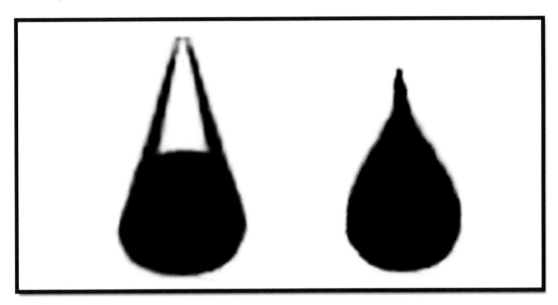

A Style and Shrunken A Style that I use

I mean I remember reading article after article in old APJ's that noted you never breed two deep rollers together because they would create roll downs. This mentality happened often when Pensom lived in California and with this way of thinking no wonder Pensom could make money doing what he did for others.

Now getting back to Bill Pensom coming to my loft and blindly judging my rollers.

Bruce Cooper notes that Pensom talked about "back muscle" and as we know now rollers don't have any significant back muscle that is used while rolling or even flying. We discussed this in a past issue of Spinner Magazine. Maybe part of Pensom's grading was really based on the eye sign, but just never mentioned it as such? This was his "hidden trick" which could be the "clusters" I mention above, but does not want to reveal this "trick" because others would see it too. Kind of like a magician revealing his trick to the world. They only mention handling the birds and then ranking them, again from someone that has never seen these birds fly or perform you need to remember.

Let's say for example that all your birds are a similar type and very related to one another but this type is something that Pensom thinks is junk. How do you think he will rate them and what will he tell you about them after you pay him for grading your birds? Will you still get an honest assessment?

I have never heard anyone speak badly of Pensom, so what was his motivation be to go around and grade rollers and assist in pairing them up for you? No one is going to travel out of their normal surroundings and do this sort of thing for fun. I can say maybe if it was done while attending a show or while at a club gathering with some bringing birds to him, but going around to other lofts with this purpose must have been a PAID service for him.

Like with me if I am selecting stock birds by the same standards to qualify for the stock loft and all were equally as good in the air (except some deeper than others) than what can Pensom really say about them that you don't already know? I can see on a trial basis that you can try something he says and see if it works but like Bruce Cooper says in the end "I am not going to present Bill Pensom as the Messiah of roller pigeons, or that everything he says or has said should be inscribed in stone." Bruce goes on to argue that Pensom has done a lot of good things for the hobby and for the betterment of the Birmingham Rollers everywhere and we know this is true, but I also know based on what Howard McCully said of Pensom that he also bred at least 500 birds annually, from 50 or more pairs, in a world where the birds of prey was not an issue like they are today. This is not counting the other kinds of pigeons he kept also.

By the same principles I know that just because you got birds from the Pensom Imports does not mean these birds are of the same strain or family when they came from at least 23 lofts. Just like all people are not the same, or all families the same, it is also true for our roller families that we develop, they don't act the same, they don't breed the same and they don't handle the same even if they might possess the same quality of roll in them as being the best you have seen. We learn by what we do and if we work with the same birds for long enough. The knowledge we get is only the experiences we have. If we never develop rollers as a family, we will never really know the birds we are working with like we could.

If we take Pensom's trick of selecting birds on the ground to the next level it would be like having your own good rollers that are proven to be superior in the air that many have seen first-hand, but none of them are PEDIGREED PENSOM ROLLERS. You in fact bought all your foundation birds from a local pet store and it took you 10 years to develop them to what they are today. These birds perform fantastic but you are unsure of their background so they are WORTHLESS right? Do you think that just because the birds came with a nice 5 generation pedigree the birds are going to perform better than the birds you already have? Well if you think this is true, I have a bridge I want to sell you.

This same type of thinking is what finally drove Pensom to leave the Pensom Roller Club (PRC) and start up the National Birmingham Roller Club (NBRC). The idea that what the birds actually do in the air MEANS NOTHING unless they are PURE THIS or PURE THAT is all bogus.

SO BE WARNED THAT WHAT THEY DO IN THE AIR IS ALL THE MATTERS.

Dr. Spintight

Question and Answer Column

This section of Spinner Magazine is for Questions and Answers. If you would like to participate in this portion of Spinner Magazine, please feel free to send questions to drspintight@gmail.com.

Question: I can't seem to get my birds to kit very tight. I am constantly having some birds fly out and this causes others to do the same. What do I do to correct this?

Dr Spintight: There could be various reason causing this. It could be birds that are just learning to roll and scared to do it, so they will stay out of the kit. It might also be from the molt and again the feathers are hurting it so if it stays out of the kit it won't roll and not hurt. It could also be a pair or several pairs of birds in your kit are PAIRED up and the cocks are trying to lure the hens down to the kit box so they can court them. So these are the main reasons that can cause this to happen in my opinion.

The young birds might have been trained too late and did not get the discipline needed to kit tight.

So the normal thing is to pull a bird from the nest at around 4 or 5 weeks old, trap train and roof train over the next 2 or 3 weeks and then get them flying at around 8 weeks old. Some guys have a hard time getting this process going timely and this will cause the birds to develop poorly I find. This is not set on stone of course but the issues always arise when birds don't have the discipline to fly and because they have matured a bit (3+ months old) they are more reluctant to the training. Some might even start to develop their sex before they are flying and this will greatly hinder their ability to get up properly.

I see some doing this and they end up culling a lot more birds than they need to just because they are not getting the birds out quickly enough to fly. The birds need to rely on each other in the kit, wanting to be with each other while flying in this "scary" world they are new to. These things is what causes them to kit tightly.

Some are just born with the "LAZY" gene and will not do what is needed or desired. You need to refrain from breeding from birds that roll good but don't kit and birds that are not a "TEAM" oriented bird. These birds don't care about coming down on their own or even landing on a telephone pole or neighbors house until the rest of the kit lands. These are REAL culls and need to be disposed of or you will never get rid of this problem with your kit birds.

Hope this helps you in your program.

Question: I have a great hen that is a very poor laying bird. She will lay very erratically and you can't really depend on her to lay when you need her to. What do you think is the problem with her?

Dr Spintight: Well there could be a lot of things going on here and it's pretty much impossible to pin it down without more information.

I have had birds as young birds lay poorly and I had suspected it could be a hormonal issue and if you foster some good eggs to these birds a few times, it will sometimes jump start their systems.

I have had other birds that started out laying great and then became erratic over several years and I think this is mostly likely a latent illness that is lingering in their sex organs. This is a bacterial infection inside the oviduct. This is most likely Paratyphoid and due to it being inside the organ is harder to treat.

I have heard from some to use Baytril pills on these birds and treat them when the bird appears to be ready to lay when mating with a cock bird. Usually within 10 days of mating up they will get "eggy" and this is the time you want to treat with the Baytril pills. The suggested dose is a pill for around 5 days in a row.

Like all use of antibiotics you will want to treat the hen with a friendly bacteria builder after treatment.

There could be an iodine deficiency which is easily corrected and worse-case scenario it might be from Inbred Depression, or some sort of genetic defect that is the issue for the specific bird.

Sorry I could not be of more assistance but this might give you a direction.

Question: I am having a hard time telling birds apart in my kit with many that look the same, what can I do that will allow me to mark the birds so they can be evaluated properly?

Dr Spintight: This is really not a big deal. I have used colored hair spray over the years with good success. You can easily obtain these hair products from a "super store" type of wholesale seller that most places have locally or online with places like Amazon. The best time to get them is just after Halloween at most retailers. I like the hair spray because it's not permanent and will fade very quickly especially if you give the birds a bath. You just wan to make sure to open the wing up fully and do several light sprays in the areas that will show up the best so it will dry well.

I like to use Yellow, Green, Red, Orange and even black works. The black works good on recessive red self. Lighter colors don't work well on black self however like some might envision.

The hardest color to mark is black self and I find if you use some scissors you can clip about 1 inch off a few tail feathers that are side by side and this will help until you find the right bird. You would also use a short piece of masking tape for this and then pinch it on the top and bottom of a specific tail feather so you can spot the bird. This is also a short-term trick that works well.

You can also tie construction flagging PVC tape around the birds' leg band by trimming it with scissors. This non sticky tape goes a long-ways but it's a little dangerous to use because they have the possibility of getting the tape hung up on something in the loft. You don't need a long piece but it will need to be around 3 to 4 inches and then you use the scissors to cut the tape narrow for about 3 of the inches on one end from the taper something like this below.

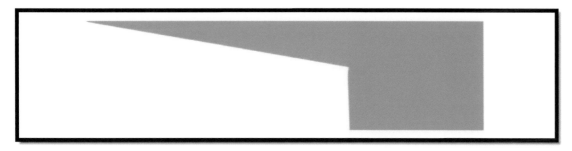

Bright Green Flagging Tape cut to tie around leg band

The pigeons have oil on their feathers and the only way to give a permanent color on a birds' wing is to strip off this feather oil first with a soap or dish soap and then use food coloring to dye the feather after. The feather will be very wet and it's best to let the wing dry before you fly the birds. It will fade over time but will remain colored for a long period of time.

I don't like this method because it stays and once you mark a bird I would use a specific color snap on band to identify birds that were performing good so you know these are done so you can move on to others. Some use 2 colors or more so when they look in the kit box they can identify the good spinners that are good enough for the "A" team from sight and know if others maybe coming in to the roll and others that might not be rolling at all yet.

Hope these ideas can assist you.

Great Finals Nor Cal – Steven Butler 2nd Place Overall 2019
L to R; Gene Barbour, Daniel Foster, Steven Butler and Judge Ferrell Bussing

NBRC 2019 TOP 5

20 Bird Final

Judge: FERRELL "IRON MAN" BUSSING

Name	Region	Depth	Quality	Score
DENNIS BLACKMORE	5	1.4	1.6	730.24
STEVEN BUTLER	9B	1.2	1.4	532.56
RICKY GONZALEZ	7B	1.3	1.5	468.0
RICK SCHOENING	8C	1.4	1.7	368.9
KEVIN MONROE	6C	1.2	1.7	352.92

11 Bird Final

Name	Region	Depth	Quality	Score
DENNIS BLACKMORE	5	0.0	0.0	408.0
OLGA MEE	8B	0.0	0.0	394.0
DON GREENE	2A	0.0	0.0	377.0
FRANK GABRIEL	1C	0.0	0.0	341.0
RUBEN SOLORIO	2B	0.0	0.0	307.0

More Info Contact
Jorge Correa
562-587-3048
rolldown4@yahoo.com

Members
Jorge Correa, Efren Lopez, Salvador Mendez, David Lopez,
Keith London, Arnold Jackson, Albert Villa, Art Martinez,
Hector Coya, Alex Otero, Maurilio Hernandez, Robert Arinas,
Ronie Williams and Jonh Jay

Promoting the Birmingham Roller hobby - competing in all major fly events; World
Cup, NBRC Fly and All Southern California Flys

In The Spotlight

Interviews in the hobby

Meet Arnold Jackson

I am Arnold Jackson and I am 77 years old and live in Santa Fe Springs, California

Do you fly with a specific roller club?

In 2008 I made a commitment to fly Kit competition. Prior to that I was flying the individual performance. At that time the BRU concept really piqued my interest. I didn't even have a team at the time, but I knew that I had to fly in this competition. Currently I'm flying with the TPRC-Top Performance Roller Club in the Los Angeles Area (2015-

present). Prior to, I was in QSDC Magazine Competition. Also our team, The Wrecking Crew, participated in all Fly's in Southern California with a high success rate. (2011-2014)

Some of Arnold's old-line birds

How would you describe your current rollers in terms of their backgrounds?

My present stock consists of a combination of my old hardcore 514 line of pigeons and a family of great competition roller pigeons from my friend Art Martinez, whose family goes back to the old Pensom Family of rollers through Danny Courtney.

What qualities can you say you are breeding for? Are you getting these qualities in your current birds?

Presently I am breeding for kit sensitivity and frequency. My family of birds maintain these qualities. My track record from my breeding has resulted in 2nd and 4th place in the California Classic (2015), Iron Man Club Champion, Put Up Shut Up Fly top 2 teams in 2014 and 2015, Battle of the Clubs top flyer for TPRC, 2nd in the World Cup for the United States, and 6th in the world in 2015.

Are you still experimenting with other birds or are you satisfied with the birds you currently have?

A: I'm racing homers just as a hobby. I'm very satisfied with my current roster.

What are your current roller friends? How long have known them?

Marshall Duncan, Art Martinez, Efren Lopez, Keith London and Johnny Smith just to name a few. I've known these guys throughout my career.

How do your birds develop? Describe how they develop in details and what percentage of roll downs do you see on average?

My young birds, with proper training, are kitting within 5-10 days in the air and will start preforming somersaults immediately. They start rolling together within a month of kitting with short rolls between 3-5 feet and steady progression between 20-30 feet within 3-4 months. 1-2% of roll downs per season.

Do you get bad losses to the BOP where you are?

A: Yes. Perigean, Cooper, Red Tail, Sparrow, Sharp Shin and others including Skunks, Raccoons, Possums, and Cats.

Have you seen this New Castle virus going down there? Thoughts?

Yes. We have been under quarantine since June of 2018. Hopefully the quarantine will be lifted by June 2019.

What has been your best breeders for your current family of rollers?

Best breeder cock bird in my loft would be TPRC-15 # 589. Dark check mk white flight. He is my most outstanding performer for quality and depth with high velocity as a booster. Truly a loft builder. My # 1 hen bred by Art Martinez is a dark check mk mixed wing who is an outstanding breeder. This is currently the base of my family of pigeons. These birds have a great work rate with sensitivity and quality in the performance.

Do you keep several families of rollers at your loft and then cross them to each other?

No

How many birds do you breed each season from how many pairs?

I breed from 12 pair, and ill raise anywhere from 60-80 birds a season.

Some of Arnolds young Birds

**I want to thank Arnold for taking the time to do this interview and he has been a real pleasure to work with on this. I would have liked to include more details but considering the space constraints of this magazine this works out great.

I know we will continue to see Arnold a top the Leadership boards in the future.

National Birmingham Roller Club

—Founded 1961

2018-19 Officers

President
DON MACAULEY 14
702-638-0915
macsrollers@yahoo.com
LAS VEGAS, NV

Vice-President
JOHN L KELLY 6A
903-245-2030
johnkelly12754@yahoo.com
BULLARD, TX

Secretary-Treasurer
JAY ALNIMER
440-258-2909
jaystarroller@yahoo.com
ELYRIA, OH

Publishing Editor
ROBERT L SIMPSON 1D
828-713-5148
NBRCPubEd@aol.com
SKYLAND, NC

National Fly Director
DON MACAULEY 14
702-638-0915
macsrollers@yahoo.com
LAS VEGAS, NV

Accessory Director
DANNY STURGEON 5
dannysturgeon@gmail.com
MADISON, MO

Band Secretary
GENE GIEGOLD 8B
805-522-7363
cpbw56@hotmail.com
LAKEWOOD, WA

Publicity Director
CAMERON DAYANAGAN 13
808-372-6251
NBRC808@gmail.com
EWA BEACH, HI

Director at Large
JON FARR 8C
wishiwon2@yahoo.com
DUBOIS, ID

Representing the Hobby for 58 Years

All England Roller Club

The All England Roller Club was formed in 1964 after talks between some of the top fliers of the time. The aim of the club is to promote through friendly competition the breeding and cultivation of high quality performing roller pigeons based on ideas developed by the founder members.

Fly Secretary Donna Chantry 01274 770668
aerc@blueyonder.co.uk
www.allenglandrollerclub.co.uk/

Voluntary or Involuntary

How many times have we been flying our kits and suddenly we see a bird or two starting to fly out of the kit for unknown reasons when it had never happened before this point? You try to figure out what bird this is and you soon discover that this bird is starting to roll and appears to be either flying just a little above the kit is or away from the kit but following them, but far enough away that it's considered out. This bird is AFRAID of the roll and this is the way it is dealing with this control issue, because when it's in the kit it will have a greater URGE to roll but not when flying by itself. This type of behavior deals with the title of this article that I hope you will find very though provoking.

These issues happen a lot but many don't really think about it and after a few times of identifying birds like some might even consider culling these birds, when a better idea would be to place a bird like this in a brand new kit of babies that has not yet started rolling, or even locking down for a period of time to mature a little.

The old timers, Pensom Era guys, had similar issues and some actually did try to "retard" the birds by not even training them until the birds were through the juvenile molt. This was a way to keep them from developing too early, because as the birds mature physically and mentally, they are better equipped to control the roll with a little age on them. I find this to be a poor method of manipulation because you will end up culling even larger numbers of birds because they don't get flying well enough, especially the young cock birds that are sometimes starting to get sexed already.

This article was somewhat provoked with a discussion I had with a friend of mine that feels the entire act of Rolling is Involuntary and we as a breeder has very limited ability in controlling it and I have nearly an opposite opinion that he had in many respects.

There has been a lot of talk over the years about if our Rollers roll from a voluntary or involuntary condition. Years ago it was thought to be a seizure or a form of epilepsy we were perpetuating in our Rollers. This topic has been a big grey area if you ask me and it appears to be a bit of both to some degree or another in my opinion, depending on the stage of development the birds are in at specific times.

I have had Rollers for over 30 years and have seen how birds develop and very seldom do I have birds that go from not rolling at all to spinning 30 feet overnight and the ones that I have had like this, generally speaking, become a Roll Down or cull in no time at all.

The normal development I would say is a bird going from sometimes tail riding or single flips then to short consecutive rolling and then graduating to a faster roll or spin within several weeks or months and gradually gaining more depth another specific time frame that is left up to the bird. This entire process can take as little as 3 or 4 months or as long as 10 to 12 months or more to fully mature into the roll as an adult bird.

I have seen birds that appear to develop over time and then become a full-fledged Roll Down going through the normal progression of development and I have had some that did virtually nothing for 6 months of flying and then develop into a Roll Down in as little as a couple of days and everything in between. Seldom however, do I get a bird that will turn into a Roll Down that was not at least rolling a little before it did Roll Down.

It has been my experience that Rolling can be compared to a young person learning to ride a bike. The more you get on the bike the quicker you will learn to master the ins and outs of riding a bike at a very high level as a skill. This would include jumping curbs, riding wheelies and some might even enjoy it so much they get into bike racing. You can relate this to most sports similarity and you just can spot some that are naturally good at specific things and this is no different for our Rollers.

If we look at how we breed these good Rollers with breeding records we can hopefully discover some tendencies that led us to create superior Rollers. The unique thing is that it's much more important to have birds that can create good Rollers compared to good Rollers that have a low-level ability to create good Rollers. So what I am saying is the key is having high percentage pairs of Rollers that can replicate themselves. We must strive to create pairs that are like this, so record keeping is very important.

So is our ability to create and replicate these good Rollers assist with making these "rolling" more "Voluntarily" with our BEST Rollers? Many of my best Rollers appear to enjoy rolling and it almost appears they are competing against other Rollers in the same kit to be the "Top GUN" or something at times. I think the premise that we can manipulate the genetics on our birds lends me to think a "Voluntary" action can be possible, but we can't pretend that Roll Downs don't exist.

We can kind of compare these characteristics to maybe training a dog to run those obstacle courses we see on TV at times. These dogs are eager to learn how to do it and we use feed to get them to do better and a little encouragement also goes a long way with animals or Pets that we have. They want to make us happy. When a Pets develop a skill or "trick" that we like it will want to keep doing it as the Pet appears to have fun doing it, because we are recognizing the behavior and this is similar to how we select our kits for competition. Maybe the "rollers" know who are the best and strive to be challenged but how can we confirm this? We really can't but birds that react to our training and follow what we desire they stay in the best kit, if not they are moved out.

If a specific bird is not cutting the mustard and not performing like we desire or expect them to perform then we will pull this bird(s) and replace it with another bird we hope will do a better job. So we know that not ALL birds will make the cut, naturally, and we are manipulating our kits to benefit US so they will do better in competition in this case. Even if we don't compete with our birds it should be our natural desire to fly a group of birds that will do well together as a team. These behaviors are going on all the time for many of us and we don't even think much about it because it happens so often, we take much of this for granted daily.

If we take a look back at the kid learning the ride a bike, we will see some kids that want to ride a bike but will fall off a few times, injure themselves and will never ride a bike again. There are yet other kids that will take their bike skills to extreme levels and injure themselves repeatedly before they master a skill. It's a passion for some to excel at things, granted even if the skill attempting could kill them with one mishap, they keep at it. These are two extremes at each end of the spectrum and we like the ones that aren't afraid to get back in the saddle and improves their skills.

With our Rollers we are striving for low problem birds and the ones that are so skilled they do things perfectly from day one as it pertains to our performing Rollers. I know I have nothing against a bird that is able to write it's wrong to perfect its skills because the bird has passion or drive within itself to do better. A Roller that has bumped several times and injured itself and continues to want to fly is a real "drive" it has to keep doing it. So this behavior also tends to lean to "Voluntary", even with our Rollers.

Well look at this statement where I say the bird has a passion or drive to do better, but in real life it might appear to just be learning to SURVIVE and flying is just what it enjoys doing when it's locked up in a small cage for 22 hours a day. I mean even if I choose not to breed from a bird due to how it developed, I might decide to just keep flying it for the betterment of my team or for my own enjoyment. So can we say that a pigeon has the ability to learn like people do, to some degree or another? Like a kid falling off his bike and then having the desire to jump back on not long after being injured, this is similar to a Roller getting injured from bumping the loft roof and going back up after some rest and getting back at it. I think this is a valid question, right?

If we go back to a statement I quote over and over again, "Like breeds Like" then we have to assume that all of what our birds do in the air is purely genetic traits and even though we can't predict all that occurs in a specific pairs genetic traits, we act like we have the control over these things and to some degree we do, but will the pair breed like he forecast them? Hard to say without doing it, no matter what science tells us.

If we get to the heart of this article and what makes Rolling a Voluntary or Involuntary act, can look at the finer points of which I mentioned in some scenarios above.

If a Roller has the ability to correct itself and stop bumping or Rolling Down, does this mean it is a Voluntary act? I would have to say Yes it is to some degree but if you feel like this is just some sort of a "Roller Instinct" that is bred into them and that the mixing of the genes will give us a specific result then we might tend to think it's Involuntary, but is it really? But why do some do this and never recover and yet other learn to NOT do it? I know some might survive a severe bump and never fly again but we are talking about birds that obviously don't hit at full force or they would have died, but had slowed before they hit.

Why do we as flyers of these birds need to manipulate them to some degree or another, with a specific loft condition, feed, water or some other type of environmental aspect to get the better results? So does environment play in to this at all?

Involuntary tells me that the bird has NO control on what happens, but I also know that how you feed the birds and keep them will also help or hinder how your birds will perform and even how they develop. So to some degree we can make or break them even.

I mean why is it that wild Rollers (lost birds) roll less than domestic Rollers kept in a loft or kit box? Why do Rollers roll more when flown with other Rollers? This tells us that part of this equation is certainly ENVIRONMENT, right? Putting a Roller in a condition or ENVIRONMENT that will encourage it to perform better and more often. This is the type of control we have as a flyer or breeder of these birds.

So this really means that we manipulate our Rollers with feed and loft conditions to achieve more performance and it's not only feed/loft, but also the genetics we use and the expectations we have. The genetics is pretty simple which means the birds either can do it right or they can't. It is the specific birds in our own programs, because not all Rollers are created equal. We are not ALL knowing and this means it is possible there are birds better out there that you, or even I, have never had to pleasure of seeing with your own eyes.

So I feel that how the birds develop in the air is what makes the entire act, Voluntary. If the act was not Voluntary why would specific birds try to NOT roll as outlined in the first paragraph of this article? They are fully aware that if they stay in the kit they will have the URGE to roll and if they are not in the kit this urge is greatly decreased. To me this is an awareness that a "dumb bird" should not have right? We see even wild birds learn how to get food on their own.

I like to sit in my loft and watch the birds and see how they act in their normal setting inside my separation pens that have a group of cocks and hens. I can see how they act, how they fly and if you pay close enough attention to these behaviors you are able to see subtle things with birds in this environment. I see birds that appear to be like sit on my perch and leave me alone, some that like to cause chaos, some that like to pair up with others of the same sex and I even notice some that are MORE ATHLETIC than others. I know part of this could be the age of the specific bird because just like people, OLDER people tend to be less athletic then teenagers or young adults and our pigeons are the same. These birds have more awareness of their surroundings also.

So what I am saying it's this AWARENESS is very natural for our best birds they obviously are under control of what they do. They start and end the roll with their awareness of their surroundings and in part this is a controlled effort. Many will not roll if they are too close to an object or not flying high enough to feel comfortable and we see these things happen often in our kits and with our kit birds.

If the birds are flying in heavy wind and can barely get to 100 feet up many of the birds will not perform in these conditions but many also will and do. These birds are just LESS aware than the others and this is also CONTROL that the birds develop or don't develop. This is why I think we need to select the best ALL AROUND birds for stock, they do it all to a high level, but we also need a few of the one wild ones. What I mean is a few that are just a little on the HOT side. We have to learn how to work with our family of birds and how to keep them going and not become too controlled or lacking control, a balanced type of bird.

We know that there is a specific TYPE we are looking for; birds that roll a lot, perform fantastic flawless spins and love to fly and kit and that anything else is just not good enough. We also know that many of our best BREEDERS are not the best performers so how do we find our best stock birds? Our entire system or breeding programs is with trial and error. EVERY year is considered a WORK in progress because if it was easy, we would all have World Class Rollers every year. This means we must experiment with birds that might have good genetics even if the specific bird is not your best spinner but has everything else you like in terms of TYPE. It doesn't always work but it's the task to experiment with specific birds that makes everything fun and exciting.

I know it is kind of hard to stay on topic here but I am just trying to put out scenarios that tell us about our Rollers and you can make up your own mind of whether Rolling is a Voluntary or Involuntary.

I just know that it's a combination of traits are Voluntary (controlled) and Involuntary (Not Controlled) that our Rollers possess. There is also environmental factors that can cause birds to lose control and perform Involuntary acts to include poor diet and flying to much as major factors in this. I mean anyone can cause birds to Roll Down and I know this is not something that a bird would want to do, meaning hurting or killing itself.

I have found some South African I have some will become frequent flippers at around 2 months old. I have tried to save them from being culled anyway I can just to preserve more kit birds to fly. What I discovered is when I find a bird doing this it's best to pull the bird from the kit for 4 weeks and lock it up. Once the 4 weeks is over the bird pretty much goes back to normal so there is some sort of "maturity" happening in the bird I feel over that 4-week period. I have tried resting for 2 weeks or 3 weeks and even less and it doesn't seem to help, the bird will keep at it, but 4 weeks seems to be the magic number on these. I am not saying it saves them all but I would say it saves 5 out of 6 birds that develop like this and the more I can save for my kit the better I am in the end.

Now if I continue to fly these birds they will start to stay out of the kit and lot and are rolling so frequent that they will eventually tire and come down and land on their own. You have to pull them from the kit within a couple days of doing this or you can risk them getting bad habits of landing early and staying out of the kit too much. Once the bad habits set in they are hard to break them of these and they will even start landing places like neighbors houses, telephone poles etc. You have to keep an eye on them and pull the specific bird before it gets these bad habits I mention or it's junk anyway.

Interesting enough though if you pull the bird move it to a holding loft where it can exercise and fly around it will forget it was doing this behavior and then you can just work it back into your kit again. It might be a little stiff but if you hold it back until the kit is has been flying a while and is just on it's way down with less than 20 minutes of flying left in the kit and you toss the bird up it will begin flying with the kit and in a few days will be able to keep up again without incident.

I think the issues arise when you have a lot of kit birds and don't have the time to mess with birds that cause problems like this. So how is a bird like this able to "fix" itself with just a little rest if it was not a mental maturity or voluntary act? Birds starting to bump or Roll Down is a little different and I find a large part of the problem is the birds like to eat a single grain and this creates a condition that makes them malnutritioned, even though they are eating everyday their body is literally starving. This is because it lacks amino acids to maintain proper health and a single grain will no give them the correct number of amino acids to sustain good health and his is what makes the birds get to a weakened state where they will start Rolling Down or doing other things that will make you have to CULL this bird.

We need to pay attention to why things happen and if you use a mixed grain and pay attention you can correct a birds' eating habits before it becomes a problem. Many birds will get used to eating a single grain when you feed a mix and they are fairly easy to spot, because they are acting much hungrier than the average bird. Like I said above if you keep too many birds you will never discover these issues that can be many times corrected and can save you a good kit bird(s) for your flying season.

I just think there is too much there in our best birds to say Rolling or Spinning is an Involuntary act and I hope that many of the factors I brought up will confirm this to you as well.

I would enjoy hearing your ideas on this topic so please feel free to email me or contact me on Facebook anytime.

Printed in Poland
by Amazon Fulfillment
Poland Sp. z o.o., Wrocław

51586630R00047